Yorkies
Today

ANNE FISHER

RINGPRESS

To my husband Bob and our three children, Jane, Robert and Christian, for their unfailing love and support, and to the memory of my father, John Newman Rayson, and brother, Jim. Above all, I would like to dedicate this book to the little dog that has made it all possible – the Yorkshire Terrier.

Published by Ringpress Books Ltd,
Spirella House, Bridge Road,
Letchworth, Herts, SG6 4ET

Discounts available for bulk orders
Contact the Special Sales Manager at
the above address. Telephone (0462) 674177

First Published 1992
© 1992 ANNE FISHER

ISBN 0 948955 77 5

Printed and bound in Singapore
by Kyodo Printing Co

CONTENTS

Foreword   5

Introduction   6

Chapter One: The History of the Breed   7

Chapter Two: Yorkshire Terriers in Great Britain   14

Chapter Three: Yorkshire Terriers in North America   28

Chapter Four: Yorkshire Terriers in Europe   37

Chapter Five: Yorkshire Terriers Worldwide   46

Chapter Six: The Breed Standard   52

Chapter Seven: The Companion Yorkie   66

Chapter Eight: The Brood Bitch and Stud Dog   79

Chapter Nine: Pregnancy and Whelping   89

Chapter Ten: Rearing a Litter   97

Chapter Eleven: Grooming and Bathing a Show Dog   105

Chapter Twelve: Training and Exhibiting   117

Chapter Thirteen: Judging   127

Chapter Fourteen: General Health Care   132

Chapter Fifteen: Yorkie Re-homing   140

Chapter Sixteen: British Champions   145

Acknowledgements

I would like to acknowledge the help of breeders and friends all over the world who have helped me so much to write this book: Vera Munday (Yadnum), who was willing to give her time and encouragement, and allowed me to use the photo of her beautiful Yorkie on the front cover; Les Griffiths (Beechrise) searched out many photographs and old catalogues; Betty Whitbread (Brybett), who lent me every photograph that she has collected over twenty years; Mary Anger (Gerardene) went through her attic to find photographs that she thought I might need; Daphne Hillman (Yorkfold) wrote the Foreword and was a mine of information; my close friend Shirley Davies (Shianda), who I always knew would be willing to come at a moment's notice if I needed her.

To the many breeders in this country who forwarded selections of photographs and information – Dave Springford, Mary and John Hayes (Chantmarles), Douglas and Hannah McKay (Clantalon), Osman Sameja (Ozmilion), and numerous others. My vet, Michael Ng, who checked my copy concerning health matters and to whom I will always be indebted for his work over the years.

To friends old and new from abroad: Jesus Montero (Coramonte, Spain), who has become our very dear friend; Heidi and Roman Alruan (Highclass, Germany) for their work in compiling information for me; Ronny and Maria Engelen (Of Millmooor & My Precious, Belgium) for their kind co-operation with photographs; Barbara McAllister Leandro (USA), Jean Bradley (USA), Suzette Heider (USA) and Bernie Brearley (Australia).

Lastly, sincere thanks to Julia Barnes, a 'hands-on' editor, who has always been available with her expertise and has permitted me to write this book in my own style.

Foreword

 This new book *Yorkies Today* is delightfully refreshing. Written with much care, it gives a real insight into the true, gritty little tyke that rules so many people's lives, whether as a beloved, faithful, family friend, or as what may appear to be a much pampered and cosseted show dog. Without fear or favour, Anne Fisher has undertaken a great deal of research and has gone to a lot of trouble to present the people and their lines that have helped to mould the breed all over the world, thus making them come alive, rather than just appearing as names on a pedigree. Anne has covered all the more general topics, such as breeding, rearing and grooming, and illustrations abound, but it is also good to see credit being given to those admirable helpers who re-home and care for Yorkies who fall on hard times, due to some crisis, however unforeseen.

Daphne Hillman,
Yorkfold, 1992.

Ch. Yorkfold Johnstounburn Gold Link (UK). (Ch. Yadnum Regal Fare – Johnstounburn Buttercup).
Bred and owned by Daphne Hillman.

Lionel Young.

Introduction

In this book I have tried to clarify and simplify the intricacies of the Yorkshire Terrier, for pet owners, aspiring show exhibitors and novice judges. The best advice I can give to anyone is to approach the breed with humility – very difficult for those who have bred other breeds, or have owned other breeds with great success.

The Yorkshire Terrier is one of the most difficult breeds to show and judge, but perhaps one of the easiest to live with. For me, they are the epitome; they think they can conquer the world. They are totally fearless: a large dog in the body of a small toy dog, loyal to the end.

The more one learns about this delightful breed, the more fascinating they become. A renowned all-breed judge once said to me that she had reached saturation point in learning about her breed. Would that this were possible with Yorkies! I have never known a Yorkshire Terrier specialist state this point of view, for the more we learn, the more we realise how much there is to learn.

Anne Fisher.

Chapter One

THE HISTORY
OF THE BREED

There are many theories as to the origin of the Yorkshire Terrier, and by studying all the information that is available from the early days of the breed and then looking at the Yorkie today, we can, to a certain extent, see how the Yorkie evolved. Before 1750, most people worked in agriculture, and then great changes began with the Industrial Revolution. In Yorkshire, small communities sprang up around the pit heads, textile mills, and factories. Workers were often badly paid, and children were forced to work very long hours from a very young age, never learning to read or write. People were drawn from as afar afield as Scotland, hoping to get work in the pits or factories. They brought their families with them, and their dogs. A breed known as the Clydesdale or Paisley Terrier was then popular with the coal miners from the River Clyde area of Scotland. It is now extinct but it was reputed to be very similar in colour to the blue and tan of the modern Yorkie. Inevitably, these dogs must have been crossed with the terriers in Yorkshire. These terriers were primarily working dogs, catching rats and rabbits, and much larger than the Yorkie that we know today. Gradually, over a period of years, these terriers were crossed with other types of terrier, probably the English Toy Terrier with its well defined colours of black and tan, and the Skye Terrier.

These dogs were certainly a working man's dog, and I think that it is fortunate for us that this was the case. Yorkshiremen have always been renowned for having an eye for a dog, and they were dedicated in their quest to breed the perfect specimen, whether it was a Whippet, a terrier or a racing pigeon. The terriers were bred down in size, and much finer bone was introduced, until a refined toy terrier finally emerged. Many people think that the Maltese Terrier was also used in the breeding at some point. I am inclined to agree with this, as not only does the Maltese Terrier have a long coat like the Yorkie, but the texture is also similar. The outline of the Maltese also resembles the outline of quite a few of the Yorkies today. We do not possess any records in the form of pedigrees of these early terrier-cross breeds, possibly because of the poor level of literacy, but we know a great deal about the type of people who bred them. There is no doubt that these early breeders had a very clear idea of the type of dog they were attempting to produce and we can see in our Yorkies today how strongly the terrier temperament has been retained.

It was in 1865 that the famous Huddersfield Ben was born. This dog – considered to be the

Huddersfield Ben,
born 1865.
Owned by Mrs
Foster.
Bred by Mr V.
Eastwood.

The Pedigree of Huddersfield Ben

		Thomas Ramsden's "Bob"
	Thomas Ramsden's "Bounce"	
Mr Boscovitch's Dog		Thomas Ramsden's "Old Dolly"
		Eastwood's "Old Ben"
	Lady	
Huddersfield Ben		Young Dolly
Whelped: 1865		
Died: 1871		Thomas Ramsden's "Bounce"
	Eastwood's "Old Ben"	
		Young Dolly
Lady		
		Old Sandy
	Young Dolly	
		Old Dolly

father of the modern Yorkie – was bred by Mr Eastwood and owned by Mr M. A. Foster. He won many prizes in the show ring, and so he became a very popular stud dog. As time went by, it was realised that 'Ben' was stamping his type on his progeny down the generations, and he is now considered to have had a tremendous influence on the breed in setting the type. Mrs Foster's Ch. Ted, who was born in 1883, was a top winning show dog and was also considered to have been a dominant sire. Mrs Foster purchased Ted at a show in 1887 when this little dog was four years of age, and in his show career he won 265 first prizes. One of his most famous sons was Halifax Marvel, whose dam went back to Huddersfield Ben.

In 1874 these diminutive Terriers were first registered in the Stud Book at the Kennel Club, and were called 'Broken-haired Scotch Terriers or Yorkshire Terriers', and this is how they were

Ch. My Precious Joss (UK), born 1963. (Ch. Pimbron of Johnstounburn – Bonny Jean).
Bred and owned by Mrs C. Flockhart.

Ch. Pagnell Peter Pan (UK), born 1961. (Ch. Burghwallis Little Nip – Prism of Johnstounburn). Bred and owned by Mrs S. I. Groom.

referred to for a number of years. It was not until 1886 that the Kennel Club deemed that the Yorkshire Terrier had progressed and improved to the point of being recognised as an individual breed. In 1898 the breeders formed the first Yorkshire Terrier Club, which to this day is called The Yorkshire Terrier Club, as opposed to the regional clubs which were to be founded later. During these early years of the Club a certain lady was to influence the breed in a way that no-one could have foreseen. She was Lady Edith Wyndham Dawson, known to all as Lady Edith. At one point she was secretary of the club, and did much work for the improvement of the breed. Lady Wyndham would attend most of the shows, arriving with about six dogs and her kennelmaid Miss Palmer, and the chauffeur carrying a picnic basket. Later Miss Palmer, who had learnt so much from Lady Edith, started to show Yorkies under her own prefix, 'Winpal'. When Lady Edith returned to live in Ireland at the beginning of the war, Miss Palmer went to work for Mrs Crookshank of the famous Johnstounburn prefix, and so began the long list of Champions under the Johnstounburn prefix, which is still active today.

During the Second World War (1939-1945) much of the activity in the dog world had to be curtailed, due to food shortages and also because petrol was rationed for many years. Breeders continued as best they could, but it was not easy. The club recommenced its activities in 1946 with Mrs Ethel Munday of the Yadnum prefix as secretary, and Mr A. H. Coates of the Martynwyns prefix as treasurer, but it was a long, hard struggle before the breed truly started to flourish once more. The first Championship show to be held after the war was on October 16th 1946 at the Holy Trinity Hall, Portland Street, London. It was held in conjunction with the King Charles Spaniels, and the judge was Mrs Clenshaw of the Harringay prefix. There was a total of thirty-two dogs – seventy-three entries – which is a very high ratio in comparison to the shows today, proving that the breeders were determined to make it a successful show. It is amusing to look at the rules listed in the catalogue:

"CHALLENGE CUPS, TROPHIES AND SPECIALS are confined to fully paid-up members of The Yorkshire Terrier Club. No bowl or cup to be won twice by the same dog.
82. Club's Challenge Bowl: for best dog in show – £1 to be given if winner does not take possession of the Bowl.
84. Club's Breeders Challenge Bowl: for best Yorkie registered within a month of birth, and shown at least once yearly since birth. Breeder and exhibitor each to receive 10/6 to commemorate each win.
86. Chapman Challenge Cup: for best puppy bred by exhibitor and registered with the Club within one month of birth.
90. Whichells Bowl: for most perfect shaped and coloured exhibit with good quality coat, which must clear the ground. No award to be made unless exhibit is sound in shape, movement and colour.
92. Lady Newborough Cup: for dog or bitch with most perfect Terrier head."

During this era names were coming to the fore that were going to influence the breed in the future. Two ladies, in particular, were starting to dominate the show scene – Mrs Crookshank of the famous Johnstounburn prefix and Mrs Annie Swan with her beautiful Invincia Yorkies.

INVINCIA Probably the most famous of Annie Swan's Yorkies was Ch. Splendour of Invincia, who gained seventeen CCs. He was sired by Invincia Masher, who sired a number of Champions although he was not shown himself because of the war. One of his daughters was Hopwood Camelia, bred by Mrs Swan, and guided to her title by Miss Martin. Martynwyns Surprise of Atherleigh, also sired by Masher, was campaigned to his title by his owner, Mr Coates. Mrs Edith Stirk had great success with this line, with Ch. Tatiana of Invincia and Stirkeans Chota Sahib gaining their titles in 1952 and 1953 respectively, both bred by Mrs Swan. Mrs D. Beech of the Deebees affix campaigned Ch. Martini to his title in 1957, again bred by Annie Swan.

JOHNSTOUNBURN It was around 1940 that Mrs Crookshank decided that she wanted to own a Yorkshire Terrier as a pet, as her mother, Mrs Usher, had always kept the breed. One day while she was driving her car in the High Street in Edinburgh, she noticed someone walking with a Yorkie. She promptly stopped the car and offered to buy the bitch. The owner handed her Yorkie over for the princely sum of £5, which was quite a lot of money in those days. Hazy, as she was known, was a typical brood type of Yorkie, rather light in colours but with a glorious, clear tan. Mrs Crookshank had no intentions of breeding from Hazy when she bought her, but she was

Ch. Yorkfold McPickle (UK), born 1962. (Ch. Burantheas Saint Malachy – Gold Dinky of Arcady). Bred by Daphne Hillman, exported to the USA.

Ch. Beechrise Superb (UK), born 1963. (Ch. Pagnell Peter Pan – Beechrise Pixie). Bred and owned by Mrs H. Griffiths.

advised that all bitches should have at least one litter, so the search was on to find a stud dog. Fairy Prince, owned by Mr. William Bain, was at stud in Edinburgh at this time. He was out of Wee Dinky O'Sighthill and sired by Lillyhill Superb, one of Mary Lowrie's Yorkies. Subsequently the litters from these two Yorkies provided the foundation stock of the Johnstounburn kennels. During this time Mrs Crookshank was asked to go and see a bitch whose owner had died. This bitch, called Flea, had a tiny dog puppy who was so ill he didn't look as though he was going to survive. Mrs Crookshank took them both back home and nursed the puppy back to health. This puppy became Int. Ch. Mr Pim of Johnstounburn, and he was line-bred to Fairy Prince. Flea never had another litter as Mrs Crookshank considered her to be too small – Mr Pim was just three pounds when he was fully grown.

Another line in the south was Mr and Mrs Latliff's Ravelin line. Many breeders used stock from this line to improve their own dogs, including Mr Coates of Martynwyns, Mr Richard Wardill of Temujin, and Miss Noakes of Phirno. Ravelin Little Jimmy was perhaps one of the

Ch. Pretty Debbie of Yadnum UK, born 1966. (Bright Star of Yadnum – Fair Phillipa).
Bred by Gwen Bulgin. Owned by Vera Munday.

Ch. Luna Star of Yadnum (UK), born 1965. (Bright Star of Yadnum – Bonny Blue of Yadnum).
Bred and owned by Ethel Munday.

Sally Anne Thompson.

most well-known stud dogs from this kennel. As time went on other breeders emerged who were to become household names in the Yorkie fancy. Mrs Flockhart, from Scotland, bred Ch. My Precious Joss, out of Bonny Jean and sired by Ch. Pimbron of Johnstounburn, a Yorkie who influenced our breed so much. Mrs Stirk with her Stirkean Yorkies, founded on the Invincia line, was a very formidable lady, especially when she was judging. I can remember her saying at one time when she was officiating: "Where is the tan on your dog – under the box?" Mrs Marie Burfield was well-known for her beautiful Buranthea Yorkies, including Ch. Buranthea Saint Malachy and Ch. Buranthea Angel Bright, who was exported to Mrs Jean Gordon in the USA, along with Ch. Buranthea Doutelle. The Burghwallis kennel was owned by Mrs Betton, and when her Ch. Burghwallis Little Nip (grandson of Ch. Splendour of Invincia) was put to Prism of Johnstounburn, the result was Ch. Pagnell Peter Pan. This was the first time that the Johnstounburn and the Invincia line had come together. Ch. Pagnell Peter Pan sired, among others, Mrs Renton's Ch. Heavenly Blue of Wiske, a Yorkie who was renowned for his gorgeous blue. From Ireland came the Clu Mor prefix, owned by the Misses Loton, who exported Ch. Starlight of Clu Mor to the USA.

The Yorkshire Terrier, both in Great Britain and throughout the world, has continued to flourish, and the early breeders who were striving to produce a diminutive toy terrier would, I am sure, be astounded at the improvement and success of this delightful breed. In 1932 only 300 Yorkies were registered with the Kennel Club in London; in 1957 the number was 2,313, and in the seventies Yorkies were the most popular breed in Britain. This trend has continued to the present day, when a record 25,665 were registered in 1990 with the Kennel Club.

Chapter Two

YORKSHIRE TERRIERS IN GREAT BRITAIN

Having written about the early days of the breed and its somewhat chequered history, we come to the modern Yorkshire Terrier. I feel that it would be useful, as well as interesting, to give some background of the kennels and dogs of today, including the characters in the breed, of which we have many, as well as the top winning Champions. It takes several generations to assess which dogs are dominant, and what they have contributed to the breed. The most famous dog in the early history was Huddersfield Ben, renowned for setting the type in the breed. Dogs such as this do not appear very often, but when they do occur it is fascinating to see how they have stamped their type on the succeeding generations. It is equally interesting to follow a line when a dog has been exported to another country, and to see how the breed has developed in a slightly different way. In the early days, breeders from overseas naturally came to Britain, the country of origin, when they wanted to start breeding Yorkshire Terriers or to improve their stock. Today the picture is a little different. In the United States and Europe in particular, the Yorkie is well established with dedicated breeders striving to improve the breed, using each other's stock as well as British bloodlines.

In Britain we are lucky in having a number of the most successful kennels still very active today, with owners who have dedicated themselves to our beautiful breed for so many years. These people are wonderful to converse with, and each one could write a book of their experiences in breeding Yorkies, as well as making the names on the pedigrees come alive for us. These famous affixes include: Johnstounburn, Yadnum, Deebees, Beechrise, Jacaranda, Phirno, Nelmila, Archambeaux, Macstroud and Dorrits, to name but a few, bringing us to the breeders that joined the world of Yorkshire Terriers at a later date, but are making their mark in the breed today to pass on to future generations. While I could sit and write about which dog produced which Champion, as many dog books do, I want to bring some of these affixes alive, to fill in the background, so that they become more than simply names on pedigrees. Some of the breeders did not, in fact, produce Champion after Champion, but they did produce dogs that have influenced the breed to such an extent that they have earned their place in history. Of course, there are so many breeders and so many dogs that it is impossible to mention everyone, but we do have more detailed histories of the breed available, and reading and researching these is a fascinating and rewarding pastime.

BARATOBA Mr and Mrs Boot founded their kennel on the Chantmarles and Typros lines, making up the bitch Ch. Chantmarles Debutante out of Chantmarles Briar Rose and sired by Chantmarles Tartar Sauce in 1979.

BEAUTARA This kennel was founded on stock from the Ozmilion and Verolian kennels and is owned by Mrs Pat Green. Her bitch, Beautara Yours Truly was mated to Verolian Emperor and they produced Ch. Beautara Height of Fashion, who gained her title in 1989, and Ch. Beautara Some Charmer in 1990.

BEECHRISE This is an affix that should need no introduction, founded by Mr Les Griffiths and his wife Hilda. They owned their first Yorkie in the late 1940s, and proceeded to breed and show to improve and perfect their stock. It was not until 1963 that the now famous Ch. Beechrise Superb was born and was crowned in 1966. This dog was out of Beechrise Pixie and sired by Ch. Pagnell Peter Pan, who was a son of Prism of Johnstounburn and sired by Ch. Burghwallis Little Nip, thus for the first time bringing together the Johnstounburn and Invincia lines. Ch. Beechrise Superb proved to be a very dominant sire, as was his sire before him, and he went on to produce Ch. Dandini Jim for Mr Blamires of the Wykebank affix, Ch. Murose Storm for Mrs E. Burton, Ch. Blairsville Aristocrat for Mr and Mrs Lister, Ch. Skyrona Blue Victoria for Mrs Sykes, Ch. Gerjoy Royal Flea for Mr Wattam, Ch. Toy Top Tango for Mrs Kitchen, and their own Ch. Beechrise Surprise. Ch. Beechrise Surprise gained eleven CCs and also sired many Champions. His most famous son must be Ch. Blairsville Royal Seal.

Many breeders have founded their kennels on stock from this line most successfully, and Yorkies the world over include the Beechrise lines in their pedigrees. Les is a mine of information about the breed, and he also takes a great deal of interest in other breeds, running a ringcraft class and judging many other breeds at Open show level. He takes a great deal of pride in how his dogs are trained for the ring, and you will never see a Yorkie from his kennel hanging back and not wanting to move in the ring – they are trained to perfection. At Crufts in 1992 Ch. Status Quo at Beechrise, bred by Mr Joe Magri out of Rozamie Emotional Desire and sired by Ch. Ozmilion Admiration, won the CC and BOB.

BLAIRSVILLE This very famous kennel was founded by Mr and Mrs Brian Lister. It was in 1963 that Brian bought his first Yorkie, a present for Rita, and this Yorkie bitch was later registered as Blairsville Lady. They were advised by their vet to mate her, and when they were searching for a suitable Yorkie to use for stud, they met Mrs Mary Henry of the Leodian prefix, who owned Leodian Smart Boy, a son of Ch. Burghwallis Vikki, who went back to the Invincia line. The mating produced Ch. Blairsville Tinkerbell and was the true beginning of the Blairsville line, which has produced many wonderful Yorkies. When Brian and Rita mated their bitch, Ch. Blairsville Shirene, to Ch. Whisperdales Temujin, it produced Ch. Blairsville Most Royale, who won eleven CCs and many top honours which culminated in Reserve Best in Show at Crufts in 1974.

The most famous Yorkie from this kennel was Ch. Blairsville Royal Seal, out of Ch. Blairsville Most Royale and sired by Ch. Beechrise Surprise, who was a son of Ch. Beechrise Superb. Royal Seal, or 'Tosha', as he was called at home, became a household name in the world of dogs; never had the ringside been so crowded as when Tosha was being shown. He was a 'King' among dogs, gliding round the ring as though his little feet were on wheels, and he could bring a

Ch. Brybett Finesse (UK). (Brybett Dedication – Brybett Brambles Wish). Bred and owned by Betty Whitbread.

Alan V. Walker.

lump to anyone's throat. In his show career Tosha won fifty CCs, all under different judges. He was twelve times Best in Show at all breed Championship shows, he totalled thirty-three Group wins, and won Reserve Best in Show at Crufts in 1978 just as his dam had done before him. This was the highlight of his career, but his unique overall achievement in the ring will be very hard to beat, and I wonder whether there will ever be another very royal Royal Seal.

BRYBETT Mrs Betty Whitbread formed this well-known kennel of Yorkies in 1966 with stock from the Martynwyns line. She first registered her affix in 1968 and has worked hard towards the betterment of the breed ever since. She was secretary of The Yorkshire Terrier Club for nearly ten years, during which time the club flourished. Betty's Ch. Brybett Finesse, who was out of the bitch Brybett Brambles Wish and sired by Brybett Dedication, a son of Ch. Ozmilion Distinction, was not widely campaigned once he had won his title. However, he was a 'classic' Yorkie, with a lovely head and expression and a lovely topline, and he always behaved like a true gentleman in the ring.

CANDYTOPS This is another of the renowned kennels in Great Britain today, founded by Mr and Mrs Oakley, based on the Deebees line. They made up their first Champion in 1973 when Ch. Candytops Blue Peter gained his title. This dog was out of Candytops Pandora and sired by Candytops Deebees Peter Piper. Many Champions were to follow, and a number of kennels have founded their stock on the Candytops line. One of the most famous of the Candytops Yorkies is Ch. Candytops Cavalcadia, who gained his title in 1981. He was out of Ch. Candytops Chantilly Lace and sired by Ch. Blairsville Royal Seal, and went on to produce Ch. Candytops Fair Delight, Ch. Wenwytes Whispers Boy, Ch. Candytops Royal Cascade and Ch. Naylenor Crown Jewel.

CARMARDY Mr and Mrs Parkin made up their first Champion in 1975, with Ch. Carmardy Little Henry, who was sired by Carmardy Captain Kydd. Several of their Yorkies have gained their title since this time, including Ch. Carmardy Annie, out of Carmardy Rose Mary and sired by Ch. Carmardy Cassius, who was made up in 1987.

CHANDAS Vic and Sue Chiswell and Sue Chiswell's mother, Mrs Leyton, were the partnership behind this line until the death of Mrs Leyton, and since then it has continued in the very capable hands of Vic and Sue. Their first Champion was Ch. Chevawn Sweet Shona in 1977, bred by Mrs Janet Campion out of the bitch Astolats Jasmine, and sired by Mogid What a Charmer from Chevawn. The Chiswells have successfully used the Ozmilion line to produce Ch. Chandas Shonas Girl and Ch. Chandas Inspiration.

CHANTMARLES This is one of the modern-day great kennels, founded by Mary and John Hayes. It all started when John bought a puppy bitch as a present for Mary, and she fell in love with the breed. Unfortunately accidents happen in the best of homes, and when the bitch was in season she escaped and was mated by a poodle. However, Mary got so much enjoyment from rearing this Yorkie/Poodle litter that she decided to breed Yorkies in a more professional manner.

They obtained a bitch, Chantmarles Mycariad Wild Silk, who was out of Mycariad Astonoff Lady Virginia and sired by Macstroud's Whitecross Dandini, and this bitch – their first show dog – became a Champion in 1968. A long list of Champions have followed, nineteen British and many others overseas. It really is a success story, and this kennel gained the award for top Yorkie in 1970, 1973 and 1980. Ch. Chantmarles Proper Madame was my favourite from the Chantmarles kennels – she was such a beautiful and elegant little lady. Ch. Dolly Dimple was always very close to Mary's heart, and if you ever ask John which one he preferred, he says without hesitation, Ch. Chantmarles Best Intention. A day that Mary and John will never forget is when, in 1971, Ch. Chantmarles Snuffbox took Best in Show All Breeds at the Bournemouth Championship Show.

There are eleven Chantmarles Champions in Canada and many in other parts of the world. One of their top winners abroad is Ch. Chantmarles Infatuation, who was exported to New Zealand and gained fifty-seven CCs for his new owner – quite a feat. Although Mary and John enjoy considerable success in the breed, they admit that things do not always go according to plan. On one occasion Mary was showing Ch. Chantmarles Snuffbox and John was holding Ch. Chantmarles Boniface on his lap at the ringside. When Mary started to walk Snuff Box for the judge, Boniface jumped off John's lap and proceeded to walk alongside Mary in the ring!

CHEVAWN Mrs Janet Campion founded this kennel, and her interest in the breed started when she picked up a stray in the street and it was never claimed. Janet has bred several Champions, but her most famous Yorkie must be Mogid What a Charmer from Chevawn. 'Jason' was one of our uncrowned Champions in the breed. He was a beautifully balanced dog, with no exaggeration in any department, and he always showed so well. I sometimes wonder if he was born before his time, as I think if he was in the ring today he would be one of the top winners. Janet says that she credits the correct colours of her Yorkies to Ch. Burantheas Saint Malachy.

CLANTALON This is a kennel that is situated north of the border in Scotland, owned by Douglas and Hannah McKay, who had their first Yorkies in the mid seventies. When they were

*Ch. Crosspins Royal
Sovereign (UK). (Ch.
Ozmilion Distinction
– Finstal Victoria).
Bred and owned by
Mr and Mrs Jim
Rigby.*

not having much luck with their first stock they asked for advice from Peter and Joyce Mann. Peter was then the convenor of the Scottish Kennel Club, and Joyce, although first and foremost a breed specialist, is also one of our top all-round judges. Joyce and Peter recommended that they contact either the Ozmilion or the Nelmila kennel. The outcome was that, after they contacted Ivy Millard, she offered them a bitch, Nelmila Berryfield Opal, grand daughter of Ch. Nelmila Berryfield Beauty. Osman Sameja offered them two brood bitches, and these were to form the foundation of their stock, bringing together two distinct lines with great success.

Nelmila Berryfield Opal was mated to Meadpark Personality Plus and produced Ch. Clantalon Contention, who gained ten CCs, one of them at Crufts in 1987. Contention then sired Ch. Clantalon Credentials, a top winning Yorkie gaining many CCs, including Crufts CC in 1991 and Reserve CC in 1992.

CROSSPINS Founded by Pat and Jim Rigby, this kennel has gone from strength to strength. They started by owning a pet bitch in 1980, and went to many shows as spectators, to watch and learn. Then they bought Bradstara Royalist, and were immediately bitten by the bug of dog showing. Their next puppy, Finstal Victoria, was bought from Mrs. Sybil Pritchard, and these two Yorkies were their foundation stock. Unfortunately for Pat, she was given some very poor advice on the care of the coat – not from Sybil Pritchard, I hasten to add. She was told to put neatsfoot oil both on the coat and in the food, and within two weeks there was no coat on either of the puppies.

This would have been enough to put most people off for life, but not Pat and Jim. They realised that they must get some expert advice and start again. The eventual outcome was that in 1987 their very beautiful Ch. Crosspins Royal Sovereign became Top Bitch, winning fifteen CCs and fourteen Reserve CCs. She was out of Finstal Victoria and sired by Ch. Ozmilion Distinction. In 1990 and 1991 Ch. Crosspins Royal Brigadier became top sire. He was out of

Crosspins Midnight Rose and sired by Crosspins Gaye Chance, and he was a dog that I always admired while he was being shown.

CYNDAHL Mrs Eileen Morris has been breeding Yorkies for a number of years with some success, particularly with Ch. Lena Alanah Snowdrop of Cyndahl, sired by Mrs Evans' Chozibar Solara and out of Cyndahl Royal Celebrity, who was sired by Bradstara Royalist.

DEEBEES Mrs Dorrie Beech founded her kennel from the Invincia line, owned by Mrs Annie Swan. Her first Champion was Martini, in 1957, who was out of Cherie of Invincia and sired by Ch. Splendour of Invincia. The Deebees Yorkies are renowned for their magnificent texture of coat and their glorious colours. Many breeders, the world over, have founded their kennels on this line. For a period of a few years in the 1980s Mrs Ann Shimwell went into partnership with Mrs Beech until Ann's very sad death. There has been a string of Champions since those early years, and Mrs Beech is still a staunch supporter of the breed. Ch. Deebees Golden Fancy gained her title in 1988; she was out of Deebees Just a Fancy and sired by Ch. Yadnum Regal Fare.

EBURACUM Mr Richard Haynes, who founded this kennel, has bred Yorkies for many years and is an expert on the history of the breed. His Ch. Eburacum Paladin, out of Eburacum Gem and sired by Eburacum Priam, gained his title in 1975.

FINSTAL Mrs Sybil Pritchard bred Ch. Finstal Sugar Baby, sired by Skyrona Blue Boy, and guided her to her title in three consecutive weeks in 1973. In 1981 Finstal Jonathan gained his title. He was out of Finstal Evita and sired by Garsims Captain Moonshine, going back to the Deebees line, and was top winning male in 1981 and won the dog CC at Crufts in 1982. After the untimely and very sad death of Sybil, Jonathan went to live with Wendy White at the Wenwyte Kennel, and a son of Jonathan, Finstal Royal Icing, was exported to the Jentre Kennels, USA, where he gained his title and became one of the top Yorkshire Terrier stud dogs of all time.

GAYSTEPS Starting with a Craigsbank bitch, sired by Craigsbank Rainlover, who was bred by Mrs Joyce Mann, I then used Chantmarles and Ozmilion stock on which to base my line. Probably my favourite show dog was Gaysteps Golden Image, who was exported to Marc Mansuet in France, where he became an International Champion. I imported Bananas du Domaine de Monderlay, who at the age of eighteen months went into quarantine at the Four in Hand Kennels at Sharnbrook for six

Ch. Bananas du Domaine de Monderlay at Gaysteps (UK).
Bred by Marc Mansuet.
Imported from France and owned by Anne Fisher.   Dave Freeman.

months. I visited her every other day to groom and cracker her coat, a formidable task, and much thanks must go to Kay and Derek Stevens, the owners of the kennels, for the fantastic care that they gave her. In the first thirteen shows that Banana was entered after the quarantine, she won six CCs and five Reserve CCs, and became the first imported Yorkie to become a Champion in the UK.

GERARDENE Founded as a mother and daughter team, Mrs Anger and Miss Mary Anger have been breeding Yorkies for many years, and are very knowledgeable on the breed history. They started with the Martynwyns line and in latter years introduced the Deebees and Blairsville lines. Ch. Gerardene Tomkins is out of Gerardene Truffles and was sired by Gerardene Troubadour; he gained his title in 1991.

JACKREED Mrs Jackie Reader has been involved in several breeds over the years, but she has always held the Yorkie closest to her heart. This line is founded on the Ravelin line and the Champions that Jackie has bred include: Ch. Jackreed Whisky A Go Go at Stewell, sired by Ravelin Little Jimmy, owned and campaigned by Mr and Mrs Bardwell in 1974; Ch. Jackreed Appleblossom, sired by Jackreed Jiminy Cricket in 1977; and Ch. Jackreed Applethyme, sired by Meadpark Personality Plus in 1991.

JOHNALENA Kathy and Ron John are the owners of this affix, and when Ron started going out regularly every weekend, Kathy began to wonder just what was going on, but she need not have worried. The only golden hair that Ron was admiring was the tan on the Yorkies' heads at the local dog shows! Soon they bought stock from Mrs Millard (Nelmila) going back to the Whitecross line. Ch. Johnalenas Silken Charm gained his title in 1981, and he was out of Nelmila Berryfield Justine and sired by Ch. Ozmilion Distinction.

JOHNSTOUNBURN In 1953 Mrs Crookshank asked Margaret Howes of the Sehow affix to join her at the Johnstounburn Kennels, and it was in 1954 that Lady of the Lake, a grand daughter of Fairy Prince and Hazy, was mated to Int. Ch. Mr Pim of Johnstounburn and produced Ch. Pimbron of Johnstounburn. Later a repeat mating produced Champions Prim and Prism of Johnstounburn. Prism was owned by Mrs Groom, and when mated to Ch. Burghwallis Little Nip, who was sired by Burghwallis Waggie, produced the Champions Pagnell Prima Donna of Wiske and Burghwallis Vikki, and at a later repeat mating produced Ch. Pagnell Peter Pan.

   The influence that these Yorkies have had on the breed is tremendous. Mr Pim himself was a very dominant sire and passed this on down to his offspring. Mary Lowrie of the Lillyhill kennel also helped Mrs Crookshank, whose health was failing at this time. Sadly, in 1960 Mrs Crookshank died, and her family asked Margaret Howes to continue the Johnstounburn prefix. Mrs Lowrie took Ch. Pimbron of Johnstounburn and Minerva of Johnstounburn, who she guided to her title. Margaret Howes was left with a daughter of Ch. My Precious Joss, and Mrs Lowrie later gave her a daughter of Ch. Minerva of Johnstounburn. With these two, and Pagnell Punchinello, a double grandson of Ch. Pagnell Peter Pan, she was able to carry on the Johnstounburn line.

KELLAYLY Mrs Gwen Kellar has been involved in Yorkies for many years, and it was in 1972

Ch. Kenandee Magic Moments (UK). (Ch. Candytops Royal Sovereign – Garsims May Be). Bred and owned by Dee Hurcombe.

Steve Wood.

that Mr John Thrupp guided Kellaylys Miss Sophie to her title. In 1974 Kellaylys Master Tino became a Champion, sired by Chunky of Archambeaux, who was owned by Mr and Mrs Darchambaud. In 1990, Kellaylys Miss Cha-Cha of Peglea, owned and campaigned by Mr and Mrs Jack Foster, gained her title. Another beautiful Yorkie from this kennel is Kellaylys Melody Maker of Willogene, owned and campaigned by Mr and Mrs Williams, who is out of Kellaylys Miss Ellie and sired by Kellaylys Tweedle-Dee. She is a most elegant bitch and a credit to the breed.

KENANDEE This small and select kennel is owned by Mrs Dee Hurcombe, who has based her stock on the Candytops line. In 1988 she guided her top winning bitch, Ch. Kenandee Magic Moments, to her title. She is out of Garsims May Be and sired by Ch. Candytops Royal Sovereign.

LYNDONEY When Doreen Johnson, who founded this kennel, bred her first litter of puppies, she thought (as we all do) that they were really beautiful and were all show types, and she was horrified when a breeder told her that they were some of the poorest quality puppies he had ever seen. Doreen was determined to learn more, and she certainly did: in 1970 Ch. Lyndoney Timothy Tuppence gained his title, sired by Little Master of Hilfore; Ch. Lyndoney Krishna followed in 1975, sired by Ch. Dorrits Macstrouds Hot Toddy; and in 1991 Lyndoney Love Affaire, sired by Ch. Ozmilion My Infatuation.

MACSTROUD Mr David Stroud is a well-known figure in any toy ring, as he now gives tickets in all breeds in the Toy Group except the Australian Silky, but he certainly didn't know what the future held all those years ago when his wife begged him to take up a hobby because he was over-working at his jeweller's bench. David decided to take a walk down to the nearest park where a dog show was being held, and there he met Jack Knight with some of his Whitecross Yorkies. Jack was about seventy at this time, and he explained that due to his failing sight, he could not drive in the dark, and this meant that he could not go to dog shows that were at any distance away. David immediately offered to drive him around the country, and he did this for the next two years.

When Jack Knight died he left all his dogs to David, of which David kept four that were to become the foundation stock of the Macstroud kennels. David is one of the founder members of the South Western Yorkshire Terrier Club and was Treasurer for some twenty-three years. He bred and campaigned a number of Champions to their titles, and many successful kennels have the Macstroud Yorkies in their ancestry, or have based their breeding on the Macstroud line – Chantmarles, Typros, Nelmila and Dorrits, to name but a few.

MUROSE The Murose Yorkies are renowned for their quality and colour. They are owned by Mrs E. Burton, who is dedicated to the breed. It was in 1968 that Ch. Murose Storm gained his title, sired by Ch. Beechrise Superb, followed by Ch. Murose Wee Pippa, Ch. Murose Exquisite, Ch. Brascaysh Bezzer of Murose, Ch. Empress of Murose, Ch. Murose Illustrious, and Ch. Murose Masterpiece.

NAYLENOR Kim and Phil Naylor campaigned their first Champion to his title in 1971. He was Ch. Brave Warrior of Naylenor, out of Sombrero Daisy May and sired by Ch. Heavenly Blue of Wiske, a dog that was renowned for his wonderful colours. The Champions that have followed include: Ch. Naylenor Blue Monarch in 1975; Ch. Naylenor Magic Moment in 1978; and Ch. Naylenor Crown Jewel in 1985.

NELMILA Ivy Millard is a wonderful lady who was secretary of the South Western Yorkshire Terrier Club for many years; both she and her husband, Pete, were founder members. Ivy is always ready to help anyone, especially novices in the breed. It was in 1957 that she first owned a Yorkie, and she later based her stock mainly on the Whitecross line. When Ivy mated Whitecross Twinkletoes (who goes back to Ch. Splendour of Invincia) to Chunky of Archambeaux (whose ancestors are mostly Ravelin breeding), the litter produced Ch. Nelmila Berryfield Beauty, a Yorkie who was to influence several kennels in the future. Another of the puppies was Nelmila Smokey Dollar, who was exported to Canada and became a Champion. Ch. Nelmila Berryfield Beauty went Reserve Best in Show at WELKS in 1969. Many kennels in the UK have benefited from stock from the Nelmila line – Chantmarles, Johnalenas and Clantalon, to name but a few, all having Ch. Nelmila Berryfield Beauty in their ancestry.

Ch. Nelmila Berryfield Beauty (UK). (Chunky of Archambeaux – Whitecross Mitzi). Bred and owned by Ivy Millard.

Cook.

Ch. Ozmilion Modesty (UK). (Int. Ch. Ozmilion Jubilation – Blairsville Bidene). Bred and owned by Osman Sameja.

Thomas Fall.

OZMILION Mr Osman Sameja became involved with Yorkies at a very young age, obtaining his first Yorkshire Terrier in 1956. However, in 1962 he still wasn't happy with the stock that he was breeding and so he went to Miss Margaret Howes of the Johnstounburn prefix, who helped him gain stock from the Johnstounburn line. Osman travelled by train up to Scotland to the Lillyhill Kennel, in order to use Ch. Pimbron of Johnstounburn at stud on one of his bitches. He selected Ozmilion Blue Orchid, a daughter of Ch. Pagnell Blue Peter and granddaughter of Ch. Pagnell Peter Pan, and this was the start of the Ozmilion Yorkies. Since those early days Osman has bred many Champions, both in Britain and abroad. He is a master of the art of grooming, and his dogs are always presented to perfection for the ring.

His Champions are too numerous to mention; however there are some that stand out. In my opinion, Ch. Ozmilion Modesty was the most beautiful Yorkie that has ever been. Bred out of Blairsville Bidene and sired by Ch. Ozmilion Jubilation, she had the most beautiful head and melting expression and was every inch a lady, unlike Ch. Ozmilion Kisses of Fire, who was very aptly named as she would not allow anyone to take liberties with her! The culmination of many years work and planning must be Ch. Ozmilion Dedication, out of Ch. Ozmilion Hearts Desire and sired by Ch. Ozmilion Admiration. Jamie, as he is known at home, gained fifty-two CCs, making him the breed record holder, and was top dog 1987. A gorgeous Yorkie, Jamie always gave his best and commanded the ring. He was a pleasure to go over, and was ever the gentleman. I speak from experience, as I awarded Jamie his fifty-second CC, after which he took a lap of honour in the Group ring under Mrs Joyce Mann. He was then retired from the show ring. The Ozmilion kennels are the top Yorkie Kennels in the United Kingdom.

PATAJOHN Mrs Pat Allington has been breeding Yorkies for a number of years with considerable success, including Ch. Patajohn Magic, out of Patajohn Merry Go Round and sired by Ch. Crosspins Royal Brigadier.

PEGLEA This well-known prefix, owned by Mrs Peggy Foster, has produced several Champions, the most famous of which must be Ch. Peglea Con Tutto, sired by Ch. Chantmarles

Sauce Box. Jack and Peggy were campaigning Con Tutto at the same time as the unstoppable Ch. Blairsville Royal Seal, and as I was always benched next to them, I know exactly how hard they worked, trailing round the circuit. Con Tutto was not the easiest of Yorkies to show, and the Fosters must be admired for how they kept him in top condition. When Royal Seal was retired, Con Tutto was the next Yorkie to be made up, having gained fifteen Reserve CCs first. Other Champions from this kennel are Ch. Peglea Salamander, sired by Ch. Beechrise Surprise, and in 1990 Ch. Kellaylys Miss Cha Cha, out of Tayfirs Jazz Me Blues of Kellayly and sired by Kellaylys Tweedle-Dee.

PITTENS A comparative newcomer to the breed, Mrs Hazel Ridgwell bred and campaigned Ch. Pittens Whisky Twinkle to his title in 1988. He is out of Gerardene Twinkle Star and sired by Copperfines Whisky Mac, and when this mating was repeated it produced Ch. Pittens Dimple Twinkle, who gained her title in 1990.

PHALBRIENZ When Brian Downey and Ralph Enz wanted to buy a Yorkshire Terrier they decided that they must buy one from the breed's original home, and so they went to Yorkshire and bought Rachelle of the Yat. However, they soon they realised that although 'Racky' was very lovable, she certainly was not show quality. They both admired the stock from the Chantmarles kennels, and it was when they bought Chantmarles President of Yat from Mrs Mary Hayes that their love of showing and breeding began. President gained his crown in 1987, and they then went on to guide Ch. Rozamie Endless Love to her title in 1988. It is the wish of all breeders to actually breed their own Champion, and this happened to Brian and Ralph when they campaigned their own Phalbrienz Tamarix to her title. She went on to win Best in Show at the United Kingdom Toy Dog Society in 1992.

ROZAMIE Mr Joe Magri, who owns this affix, has bred many beautiful Yorkies that have gained their titles both in the UK and abroad. His first success came with Ch. BeeBee Mi Blaze, bred by Mrs J. Mitchell, out of Heidi of Peppinoville of Bee Bee Mi and sired by Ch. Blairsville Royal Seal in 1983. The Rozamie affix features in many Yorkies on the Continent, along with the Ozmilion affix.

SHIANDA This small and select kennel was founded by Mrs Shirley Davies on the Deebees line. Her home-bred Champion Shianda Royal Fanfare was out of Shianda Cara Cree and sired by Deebees Othello, and grandson of Blairsville Royal Seal. Shirley is a dear friend, who has accompanied me on the many miles to the dog shows.

STEWELL The partnership behind this well-known prefix is Mr and Mrs Stephen Bardell, and Stephen's mother, Mrs Elizabeth Bardwell, and they have been breeding Yorkshire Terriers for many years. Elizabeth is the secretary of the Eastern Counties Yorkshire Terrier Club. Their line is dominantly based on the Ravelin line, and their Champions include Ch. Jackreed Whisky A Go Go at Stewell, sired by Ravelin Little Jimmy and bred by Mrs Reader, Ch. Stewell Soul Singer, sired by Stewell Sensation, Ch. Stewell Moonstorm, sired by Whisky A Go Go, and Ch. Stewell Storm Queen, sired by Moonstorm.

TAYFIRS Mrs Jean Fairbrother has been breeding Yorkies for many years, guiding Ch. Tayfirs

Firegift to his title in 1969. This dog was out of Rose of Reenad and sired by Mr Teddy of Phylreyne. Ch. Tamiche of Tayfirs, sired by Tayfirs Regal Steel, is also from this kennel.

TYPROS This kennel was founded by Mrs Gladys Da Silva on the Macstroud, Whitecross lines, and in the latter years she has used the Ozmilion line to great advantage. Ch. Typros Evening Star, out of Macstrouds Evening Star and sired by Cheeky Boy Typros, was the kennel's first Champion, gaining her crown in 1978. Several were to follow: Ch. Typros The Devil of SpiceBox, Ch. Typros Royal Splendour, Ch. Typros Lady of Elegance and Ch. Typros New Generation.

VEROLIAN Mrs Sameja Hilliard has founded her stock dominantly on the Ozmilion line, and her Champions include Ch. Verolian Temptress with Ozmilion, who is the bitch breed record holder with a total of thirty-nine CCs.

WENWYTES Wendy White, the founder of this kennel, used to breed and show horses and also Poodles. However, she felt that the Poodle temperament was not what she was looking for in a dog. A relation kept Yorkies, and she thought this breed might suit her better, never imagining that she would become totally besotted with the breed! After the sad death of Mrs Sybil Pritchard, Sybil's husband asked Wendy if she would look after Ch. Finstal Johnathan. Johnathan is an old boy now, but he still mates the occasional bitch, and he has been a great help in Wendy's breeding programme. A son of Jonathan, Finstal Royal Icing, was exported to the USA after Sybil's death. He gained his title there, and he is certainly making his mark on the breed.

It was in 1982 that Ch. Wenwytes Whispers Boy gained his title. He is out of Wenwytes Winter Whisper and sired by Ch. Candytops Cavalcadia. A lesson can be learnt here, for Whispers Boy could be a very difficult dog to show, and if the judge took too long, he would assume the most bored expression. To counteract this, Wendy used to take a little cooked liver in the ring with her, and hold it in her mouth, in case it was needed. On the day he gained his title the judge, Mrs Tuckwell of the

Ch. Wenwytes Without Doubt (UK). (Ch. Wenwytes Whispers Boy – Welcome Magic at Wenwytes). Bred and owned by Wendy White.

Dundry prefix, handed Wendy the ticket, and she was so shocked that she choked on the piece of liver! Wendy also guided Ch. Chevawn Special Engagement to his title in 1989, and in 1991 Ch. Wenwytes Without Doubt gained his title. He is out of Welcome Magic at Wenwytes and sired by Ch. Wenwytes Whispers Boy.

WYKEBANK Mr Ave Blamires and Mrs Joyce Blamires founded this kennel and bred many beautiful Yorkies. Their first Champion in 1968 was Ch. Dandini Jim, who was sired by the great Ch. Beechrise Superb. Several Champions followed, and after the sad death of Joyce, Ave married Janice Bunting, who had already campaigned a bitch, Maritoys Midnight Rose, to her title in 1985. After the untimely death of Ave – just a few weeks before he was due to judge Yorkies at Crufts 1992 – Janet has been left to carry on the famous Wykebank name, which I am sure she will do admirably.

YADNUM This famous kennel was a mother and daughter partnership – Mrs Ethel Munday and her daughter, Miss Vera Munday – until the death of Mrs Munday. It is wonderful to talk to Vera as she knows so much of the history of the breed, and she has been a great help to me in writing this book. Vera and her mother always had their own show dogs, and although Vera appeared to be in her mother's shadow, she was often the driving force behind the kennel. Ch. Wee Eve of Yadnum, sired by Int. Ch. Mr Pim of Johnstounburn, gained her title in 1952. Unfortunately she was too small to be bred from. The next Champion, Ch. Eoforwic Envoy of Yadnum (whose dam was Florentina of Yadnum, and sired by Blue Guinea of Yadnum) has a story of his own. Mrs Munday, unknown to Vera, sold Florentina in whelp. Vera was not at all happy with the arrangement, and so when the litter was ready to leave the dam, she bought Envoy back in. Ch. Midnight Gold of Yadnum gained his title in 1954, Ch. Elmsglade Galahad of Yadnum in 1962, Ch. Golden Buttons of Yadnum in 1964, Ch. Luna Star of Yadnum in 1968, Ch. Pretty Debbie of Yadnum in 1969, Ch. Superfine of Yadnum in 1970, Ch. Mycariad

Ch. Robina Gay of Yadnum (UK). (Ch. Mycariad Ragged Robin – Gay Rosalina of Yadnum). Bred and owned by Vera Munday.

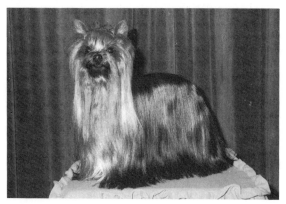

Ch. Yadnum Regal Fare (UK). (Ch. Candytops Cavalcadia – Yadnum Lovejoy of Azurene). Bred and owned by Vera Munday.

Ragged Robin of Yadnum in 1972, Ch. Robina Gay of Yadnum in 1974, Ch. Azurene Moss Rose of Yadnum in 1983, and Ch. Azurene Corduroy of Yadnum in 1985.

My favourite of the Yadnum Champions is Ch. Yadnum Regal Fare, featured on the cover of this book. Reegie, as he is known at home, is a most beautiful Yorkie with all the attributes necessary to be a 'classic'. He has a gorgeous, balanced head with lovely clear tan, and a good topline, which he always held on the move; a true gentleman in the ring, never putting a foot wrong. In fact, he is Vera's favourite too, because she says that he has always been an easy dog to get along with at home, always wanting to please. Reegie has sired Ch. Deebees Golden Fancy and Ch. Yorkfold Johnstounburn Gold Link among others. For many years Vera was treasurer for The Yorkshire Terrier Club, and she says that over the years the presentation of Yorkies for the ring has improved beyond belief. However, she feels that ring etiquette is far worse than it used to be.

YORKFOLD JOHNSTOUNBURN Daphne Hillman is a true stalwart of our breed. She became interested in Yorkies when her step-mother owned one, called Tuffy. Eventually Tuffy went to live with Daphne, and her life changed from that day onwards. She registered her affix in 1956, and has been totally involved in the breed. Luckily for Daphne, she was able to buy Prim of Johnstounburn, out of Lady of the Lake and sired by Int. Ch. Mr Pim of Johnstounburn, and made her a Champion in 1957. It was Prim's sister, Prism of Johnstounburn, owned by Mr V. Groom, who was later put to Ch. Burghwallis Little Nip to produce Ch. Pagnell Peter Pan. Ch. Yorkfold Wrupert Bear gained his title in 1963, but it was Ch. Yorkfold McPickle, sired by Burantheas Saint Malachy, who was a great show dog for Daphne, always to be relied on for never putting a foot wrong in the show ring. McPickle gained his title in 1963. He was out of Yorkfold Koala and sired by Yorkfold Chocolate Boy, and when exported to the USA he became a Canadian and American Champion.

Following the Johnstounburn line, the Yorkfold Yorkies have glorious clear tans – so much so that when Daphne exported one Yorkie the owner phoned and wanted to know how to remove the dye from the coat! Of course, many American Champions have the Yorkfold line behind them, including the Barbaranne line. In 1981 Margaret Howes of the Johnstounburn line decided she could no longer show her Yorkies due to ill health, so she asked Daphne to go into partnership with her, with the knowledge that the prefix would continue in very capable hands. In 1991 Ch. Yorkfold Johnstounburn Gold Link gained his title. He is out of Johnstounburn Buttercup and sired by Ch. Yadnum Regal Fare.

Chapter Three

YORKSHIRE TERRIERS
IN NORTH AMERICA

The first Yorkie to become an American Champion was Bradford Harry, who gained his title in 1889 when he was four years old. His great great grandsire was Huddersfield Ben, and he was imported from England from Mr W. Beal and was owned in America by P. H. Coombs of Bangor, Maine. Interest grew in the breed in the succeeding years, but it was not until after the Second World War that Yorkies were imported to the United States in any number. American breeders wanted to obtain stock from the top English kennels, and these enthusiasts were to have a great influence on the future of the Yorkshire Terrier in North America. One of the most notable is the Wildweir kennels, founded by two sisters, Janet Bennett and Joan Gordon, who imported many Yorkies from England in the early days. Their stock included several different British lines, including Johnstounburn, Harringay and Buranthea, and today kennels all over the USA and parts of Europe have the Wildweir Yorkies in their ancestry. The Mayfair-Barban kennels, owned by Ann Seranne and Barbara Wolferman, have also done much to improve the quality of the Yorkie, and still do. Ann Seranne has written a superb book on *The Joy of Breeding Your Own Show Dog.*

Ch. Cede Higgens has made history in the American show scene, winning the Top Toy award for 1978 and Best in Show at Westminster in the same year. He was shown at approximately the same time as Ch. Blairsville Royal Seal, and they were often compared, but all agreed that they were two fantastic Yorkies of totally different type. Ch. Cede Higgens, bred by C. D. Lawrence and owned by Charles and Barbara Switzer, has predominantly Clarkwyns and Wildweir ancestors, and is closely line-bred to two particular dogs. The first needs no introduction – Ch. Wildweir Pomp'N Circumstance – one of the top stud dogs in America; the other is Ch. Toy Clown of Rusklyn, who won the Dog CC at Crufts in 1960, and was bought and exported to the United States by Mrs Clark for her famous Clarkwyn kennels. Ch. Finstal Royal Icing has also had a significant influence on the breed in North America. He was bred by Mrs Sybil Pritchard and exported to the Jentre kennels after Sybil's death. A son of Ch. Finstal Jonathan, he is now one of the top sires in the United States, and I have been amazed at the many photographs and pedigrees I have seen of his beautiful offspring, sent from breeders throughout the United States and Canada. He has proved to be a truly great ambassador for the breed.

Because of the vast size of the countries, exhibitors in both the United States and Canada have

Bradford Harry.
Exhibited at
Westminster
in 1890.

Pedigree of Am. Ch. Bradford Harry

			Bateman's Sally
		Sandy	
	Bruce		Venus
		Patterson's Minnie	
Am. Ch. Bradford Harry			
Whelped May 16, 1885			Huddersfield Ben
		Tyler	
	Lady		Kitty
		Lady	

to travel long distances to shows – sometimes many thousands of miles – although a group of shows is often organised in one area on consecutive days. The alternative to travelling to shows is to employ a professional handler, who goes on a circuit campaigning several dogs. Judging is based on a points system, and dogs do not have to compete against Champions in order to gain their title; the Champions have their own class. Many exhibitors in Britain feel that we should adopt the same method. However, I have some reservations, and I think that there is much to be said for both systems. If there is a top winning dog being campaigned in Britain, then a lot of

Finstal Royal Icing as a puppy, before being exported from the UK. (Ch. Finstal Johnathan – Finstal Angel Cake). Bred by Sybil Pritchard. Owned by Ruth S. Jenkins.

Dennis Assinder.

Ch. Arriba of Arriso (USA). Bred by Peggy Harris. Imported from the UK and owned by John and Dorothy Leonard.

Bill Francis.

very worthy Yorkies are passed over and never become Champions. This would not be a problem in America, but on the other hand, it can be argued that competing against the Champions and top winning dogs ensures that the quality of Yorkies is maintained and improved upon. Perhaps a compromise between the two systems would be more ideal. It is interesting to note that, on the average, Yorkies in North America gain their titles at a much younger age than their British counterparts. In the USA many breeders now train their Yorkies for their Obedience titles. Mrs Dolores Denton from Virginia owns Ch. Tiffany's Dixie Charmer, who is reputed to be only the second Yorkie in the history of the United States to accomplish both her Show title and Obedience title. The first time this double honour was awarded was in 1945.

It is impossible to look at all the Yorkie breeders in North America, but I have tried to get a cross-section of renowned breeders and some less well-known breeders, and to cover as many different areas as I could, in order to give an insight into the Yorkie fancy.

BIANCHILANE, Ontario. Irene Bianchi (originally from the North of England) is vice president of the Canadian Yorkshire Terrier Association, and she has been breeding Yorkies for many years. Her first Yorkie bitch was Seekapetra Idealist, and she went back to the Yorkfold and Yadnum lines. In more recent years Irene has included Wildweir and Vassar Square breeding. Ch. Bianchilane Pocketful O Dreams is out of Ch. Bianchilane Annies First Fling and sired by Ch. Filagrees Professor Higgens, whose sire is the famous Ch. Cede Higgens.

Ch. Bianchilane Fame's Symbette (Canada). (Ch. Bianchilane's Symbol at Lencon – Bianchilane's Claim to Fame). Bred and owned by Irene Bianchi.

CHONDINE, New Jersey. Mother and daughter team, Claire and Lisa Pollitzer, founded this kennel on mostly Mayfair-Barban stock in 1983. In fact, their first show bitch was Ch. Fireacres Calendar Girl, bought from Sharron McCadam, but she had a lot of Mayfair-Barban in her pedigree. Claire and Lisa have made up nine Champions to date, and have handled and guided four Yorkies to their title for other people. Lisa was given her first pet Yorkie when she was eleven years of age, and she spent many years studying the breed before she started breeding and exhibiting. This has certainly paid off, as she has achieved much in a comparatively short time, and is now the president of the Watchung Mountains Yorkshire Terrier Club.

Ch. Chondine Country Connection (USA). Bred and owned by Claire and Lisa Pollitzer.

Ashbey.

Ch. Foxbrides Even So (USA). (Ch. Rawlins Kris Kringle – Christinas Silver Doll). Bred by Lyn Fox. Owned by Sharon Waldeck.

Ashbey.

Miss Whitney Blue (USA). (Ch. Jentre's Jolly Roger – Muffin March Delight). Grand-daughter of Ch. Finstal Royal Icing. Bred by G. and D. Goesch. Owned by Barbara McAllister Leandro.

Cook.

DORCHESTER, California. John Leonard and his wife Dorothy have been breeding Yorkshire Terriers since 1967, acquiring their first Yorkie from Mrs Stirk's Stirkean kennels. They are regular visitors to the UK, and they have continued to buy stock from the top breeders – Tzumiao, Deanchel, Mycariad, Ozmilion, and others. Stirkean's Tiny Tim of Kingsmere, who was sired by Ch. Stirkean's Astonoff's Horatio, won top honours in the show ring and was the first Yorkshire Terrier in America to win his International title. Many of the Tzumiao Yorkies, bred by Elsie Gilbert, were to gain their titles in America in the capable hands of the Leonards. Most of the Dorchester Yorkies today trace their ancestry back to these English Imports.

Ch. Mayfair Barban Lark (USA). Bred by Ann Seranne and Barbara Wolferman.
Ashbey.

GINSENG, Ontario. Ann Robert, who founded this kennel, started in Shih Tzus and spent some five years with this breed before embarking on breeding and showing Yorkshire Terriers. Ann bought a seven-month-old Yorkie, Shakespeares Double Delight, who goes back to Jentre breeding and has Ch. Mayfair Barban Jamoca in her pedigree. This Yorkie turned out to be Canada's all-time top winning Yorkshire Terrier, winning fifteen All Breed Best in Shows, three Best in Show Club Shows, and one hundred and seven Group wins. She was Top Toy in Canada in 1988 and again in 1989 – quite an achievement for Ann, with her first Yorkie. Delight was mated to none other than Ch. Finstal Royal Icing, and produced two puppies, who will hopefully be making a name for themselves in the show ring.

Ch. Rothby's Red Ribbons (USA). (Ch. Rothby's Rogue Royal – Ch. Rothby's Reflection).

Graham.

HEILAND, Florida. Suzette Heider, who is the owner of this kennel, is the secretary of the Central Florida Yorkshire Terrier Club. It is interesting to note that the Yorkie Clubs in the United States seem to be far more active socially than their British equivalents. The Central Florida Club has a meeting twice-monthly, which seems to be the norm for all the clubs. Central Florida's membership is drawn from the whole of Florida; although they are numerically quite small, they are working to gain full status to hold point shows. Ch. Rothby's Red Ribbons, bred by Roberta Rothenbach, is out of Ch. Rothby's Reflection and sired by Ch. Rothby's Rogue Royal.

KINTYRE, California. Barbara McAllister Leandro is the corresponding secretary for the Yorkshire Terrier Club of Northern California, and she emigrated to America from England about thirty years ago. In fact, there seem to be a lot of expatriates in the USA breeding Yorkies. Barbara has been a tremendous help to me while I have been researching this book, sending me invaluable information. The Yorkie that she is showing at the present, Miss Whitney Blue, is well on her way to becoming a Champion. She is bred by Gerald and Dorothy Goesch, and is out of Muffin March Delight and sired by Ch. Jentre's Jolly Roger (who is sired by Ch. Finstal Royal Icing, and has Candytops Jerome Bear in his ancestry).

Int. Ch. Shakespeare's Double Delight (Canada). (Ch. Shakespeare's As You Like It – Pastoral Devils Delight). Bred by Roxanne Miligan and Diane Kijowski.
 Owned by Ann Robert.

Mikron.

Ch. Stangor's European Holiday (USA). (Ch. San Crest Hug E Bear – The Wenz Sugar N' Spice). Bred by Mrs Ruby Wenz and Mrs Dorothy DeBoer. Owned by Katherine Stangeland and Helen Gordon.

Callea

STANGOR, California. Katherine Stangeland and Helen Gordon started to breed Yorkies in 1981. Their foundation bitch, Ch. Princess Tricia of Stangor, sired by Ch. San Crest Tora Tora, produced Ch. Stangors Harcourt-Smith. Katherine and Helen only breed in very small way, but it is interesting to note that one of their present youngsters, Stangors Candy Man, is sired by Vassar Square Pepper, whose grandfather is Ch. Finstal Royal Icing and whose grandmother is Ozmilion Royal Kiss.

STRATFORD, Pennsylvania. Barbara and Ron Scott founded this very successful kennel. They have had many Champions; however, there are three Yorkies that stand out. Firstly, Ch. Denaire Royal Lace, who is out of Ch. Denaire Fame and sired by Ch. Finstal Royal Icing. Royal Lace went on to produce an amazing tally of seven Champions in three litters; secondly, Ch. Mistangays Boom Boom Mancini, grandson of Royal Icing and out of Ch. Denaire Dawn at Mistingay and sired by Ch. Mistangays Angelo; and last but not least, Ch. Stratfords Magic, out of Ch. Denaire Royal Lace and sired by Ch. Mistangays Angelo. Magic is the top winning Yorkie 1991 (The Yorkshire Terrier Club of America), with one Best in Show (all breeds), two Best in Show (club shows) and thirty Group wins.

Ch. Straford's Magic (USA). (Ch. Mistangays Angelo – Ch. Denaire Royal Lace). Bred and owned by Barbara and Ron Scott.

VASSAR SQUARE, California. Terri and John Shumsky made up their first Champion, Ch. Vassar Square Gemini Teddy, in 1976. Since then this kennel has gone from strength to strength, and to date it has twenty-eight home-bred Champions to its credit, including Ch. Vassar Square Eliza Dolittle, who is a Best in Show winner. The Vassar Square Yorkies feature in the pedigrees of many kennels in North America.

YORKBORO, Washington. Doreen Hubbard founded her Yorkie kennel in 1967, and in 1973 she bought Am. Can. Ch. Mayfair Barban Jamoca as a puppy (out of Mayfair Barban Honeydew and sired by Ch. Mayfair Barban Mocha Mousse), along with two compatible bitches. In 1979 Jamoca was mated to a bitch with part-English bloodlines, and the result was Yorkboro Crimson and Clover, who was to become an American and Canadian Champion, and the dam of twelve more Champions. All Yorkboro Yorkies today go back to Clover. She is the granddam of Am. Can. Ch. Yorkboro My Main Man, in 1990 and 1991 top winning Yorkshire Terrier in the USA; and a Clover granddaughter, Int. Am. Can. Ch. Yorkboro Good Golly Ms Molly has just completed her international title in France.

KITTY GIELICZ is the secretary of the Yorkshire Terrier Club of Greater Los Angeles. Her dog, Int. Ch. Dynasty's Moonlight Bandit, was bred by Jane Ferguson, but is mostly bred from the famous 'Showoff' line owned by Beth Wayman.

Int. Am. Can. Ch. Yorkboro Good Golly Ms Molly (USA). (Int. Ch. Yorkboro Follow The Leader – Hy-Lines No Deposit No Return). Great Granddaughter of Mayfair Barban Jamoca. Bred and owned by Doreen Hubbard.

Chapter Four

YORKSHIRE TERRIERS
IN EUROPE

Due to the close proximity of Europe to the UK, many exhibitors from the Continent attend our shows as spectators throughout the year. The Yorkies in Europe tend to be slightly larger in size compared to those in Britain, but the quality is very high, with dedicated breeders working hard to improve their stock. As they are not restricted by quarantine laws, exhibitors can travel to compete in many different countries, and I believe this has got to be healthy for the breed, as generally, the more competition there is, the higher the standard becomes. Many of the top dogs from the Continent are taken to the USA to gain their titles there, and whereas years ago everyone had to come to Britain to buy Yorkies, now the scene has changed and breeders from Europe and America use each other's stock. I think this is a trend that will continue and grow. When I have visited Europe, either to judge or simply as a spectator, I have found it fascinating to study the pedigrees and see how the breed has progressed. There was a somewhat dramatic change when the Yorkie was switched from the Toy Group to the Terrier Group – a move which I heartily disagree with. It has led to Yorkies becoming bigger in order to compete more equally against the larger terrier breeds. I can see that it must be very difficult to compete against an Airedale, but what a pity that Yorkies were moved in the first place! The Yorkshire Terrier is a toy terrier, and it should not be bred to be larger, simply to suit the Group it belongs to. If breeders start to worry too much about Group identity, the breed in question will lose its own identity. Not all of the countries have official Yorkshire Terrier Clubs; some come under the umbrella of their National Club with their own representative, for example Norway, which has an annual registration of about fifty Yorkies. Judging methods are different in Europe compared to the UK and the USA. One of the main distinctions is that there must be a minimum period of a year between a dog winning its first CC and its last CC, and this can present a number of problems for exhibitors. For instance, a Yorkie that is light in colour when winning its first CC is unlikely to hold that colour for the mandatory year before attempting to win its last CC. And in most European countries both dogs and bitches must be shown and win a certain grade in a special breeders class, before they can be bred from and register the puppies.

In this chapter I have included prefixes from as broad a cross-section as possible. Obviously there are many that have had to be left out, for which I apologise, but there are hundreds of Yorkie breeders based in many different countries.

Ch. Barry of Anasor (Holland). (Int. Ch. My Precious Clide – Justimagine of Anasor). Bred by J. Cranebroek. Owned by M. Rensson-Mols.

ANASOR, Holland. The owner of this kennel is no stranger to the UK show scene. Mr J. Cranenbroek has been breeding Yorkies for many years and founded his stock on the Deebees and Kellayly lines from England, and also the Of Millmoor stock from Belgium. Ch. Barry v. Anasor is sired by Int. Ch. My Precious Clide out of the bitch Justimagine of Anasor, the grandsire is Deebees Gold Digger and the granddam is Kellayly's Mandy Blue.

BAJAZZOS, Germany. This kennel is situated close to Hamburg and is owned by Rudi and Walli Hodl. They have founded their stock from the Highclass kennel of Roman and Heidi Alruan. Rudi and Walli are very dedicated breeders, and their Champions include Ch. Highclass Royal Star, out of the bitch Highclass Justine (who is Johnstounburn breeding) and sired by Ch. Highclass Royal Seal, son of Blairsville Royal Seal. Ch. Bajazzos Mandy is an exquisite bitch, sired by Highclass Merry Mark.

BI'ENNA, Denmark. Ib and Annelise Sorensen started breeding Yorkies in 1971, with a bitch puppy they bought from Mrs Taylor (Deanchels), and then were lucky enough to buy a litter brother of Ch. Deebees Speculation from Mrs Beech. At a later date, stock from the Candytops kennel was added, and these formed the foundation stock for this well-known prefix. They have now

Int. Ch. Bi'Ennas Touche (Denmark). (Int. Ch. Hold-Up – My Precious Lingeling). Bred and owned by Ib and Annelise Sorensen.

produced twenty-seven national and international Champions, including Ch. Bi'Ennas Touche and Ch. Bi'Ennas Lady Be Good.

BLOOMSBURY, Germany. This is another of the top kennels in Germany, owned by Mr Grunn, who has used the Of Millmoor line of Yorkies to great advantage. As with most of the top kennels in Europe, these Yorkies are always turned out to perfection and shown with great professionalism.

BONSAI, Italy. Mrs Sonia Pagani has produced many beautiful Yorkies, but perhaps her most famous is Int. Ch. Bonsai Sweet Sensation, out of Suzanne Della Zagara (who has Rozamie Twinkle in her ancestry) and sired by Ch. Get It Of Millmoor, who is the son of Ch. Ever Trouble of Millmoor. Sweet Sensation is a Champion in Italy, Austria, Yugoslavia and Germany, gaining twenty-three CACIBs in her illustrious career.

Int. Ch. Bonsai Sweet Sensation (Italy). (Ch. Get It Of Millmoor – Suzanne Della Zagara). Bred and owned by Sonia Pagani.

BOW-WOW-WOW's, Norway. This kennel, owned by Grethe Hansen, has a Yorkie in the top five Yorkies in Sweden, owned and handled by Liv Heitmann who is the Yorkshire Terrier breed representative in Norway. Ch. Bow-Wow-Wow's Miss Pia is from mostly English stock, with Ozmilion, Sladesmark and Candytops breeding, and is sired by Bow-Wow-Wow's Dark Surprise.

Ch. Bow-Wow-Wow's Miss Pia (Norway). (Bow-Wow-Wow's Dark Surprise – Ch. Bow-Wow-Wow's Penelope). Bred by G. Hansen. Owned by Liv Heitmann.

Ch. Iris of Coramonte (Spain). Bred and owned by Jesus Montero.

Rafa.

CORAMONTE, Spain. Jesus Montero, who owns this kennel, has been breeding Yorkies for many years. He is the chairman of the Yorkshire Terrier Club in Spain, and is situated just outside Madrid. He is a dedicated breeder and attends most of the shows in Spain. Jesus founded his kennel on mostly the Ozmilion line and latterly Gaysteps stock. He exported his Teo De Coramonte to Japan, where he became a Champion. Other Champions from this kennel include Ch. Iris De Coramonte and Ch. Denysse De Coramonte. There are a lot of dog shows in Spain, except in August, when they are suspended because of the heat.

DEBONAIRE'S, Sweden. Bernice Unden started her famous kennel in 1969 with mostly English stock from the Ozmilion kennel, and also Carmardy Henry from Joan Parkin. Bernice has made up over fifty Champions and fifteen of these have gained their international titles. Int. Ch. Debonaire's Believe In Music or 'Strauss', as he is called at home, was top Yorkie 1990. He is out of Int. Ch. Debonaire's Blue Carisma and sired by Ch. Henrikville The Boss. In 1991 Int. Ch.

Int. Ch. Debonaire's This Is My Music (Sweden). (Int. Ch. Henrikville The Boss – Ch. Debonaire's Blue Carisma). Bred and owned by Bernice Unden.

Debonaire's This Is My Music gained the same title. Top Yorkie in Finland in 1991 was Ch. Debonaire's Mini-Snob, and Norway's top Yorkie in the same year was Debonaire's Tip Top Tidy. Is there any wonder that Bernice is now top breeder of Yorkshire Terriers in Sweden?

DE MONDERLAY, France. Marc Mansuet founded this kennel near to Paris, and he travels throughout Europe showing his dogs. His Yorkies are line-bred to his own Int. Ch. Royal Flash du Domaine de Monderlay, a lovely Yorkie who was renowned for his fantastic movement, among his other attributes. My own Ch. Bananas du Domaine de Monderlay was bred by Marc, and was the first Yorkie to be imported into Britain to become a Champion. She is sired by Royal Flash, and she inherited his movement. Marc imported my Gaysteps Golden Image ('Teddy') into France and guided him to his International title. Teddy won one CC and five Reserve CCs in England before going to France.

Int. Ch. Gaysteps Golden Image (France). Bred by Anne Fisher. Imported from the UK and owned by Marc Mansuet.   M & S Studios.

DE PENGHIBUR, France. It was in 1965 that this kennel was formed, and Madame Gerard has bred many beautiful Champions – five French and twelve international. This includes her very famous Int. Ch. Uddersfield Ben De Penghibur, out of Talismane De Penghibur (who has Millmoor and Beechrise in her pedigree) and sired by Int. Ch. Tilbury De Penghibur (who is sired by Int. Ch. Ever-Trouble of Millmoor). Uddersfield Ben is also an American Champion, and he really is an outstanding Yorkie. Madame Gerard is a very dedicated breeder and supports shows in many of the countries on the Continent.

World Ch. Uddersfield Ben de Penghibur (France). Bred by Marguerite Gerard. Exported to the USA to Kathleen B. Kolbert and Richard S. Lawrence, to gain his title.

Int. Ch. Highclass Royal Magic Moment (Germany). (Highclass Royal Prince – Highclass Minette). Bred and owned by Heide and Roman Alraun.

HIGHCLASS, Germany. Situated near Neustaad, this kennel was founded by Roman and Heide Alraun, and it is one of the top kennels in Germany. I say 'kennels' but, in reality, most of their Yorkies are much-loved house pets. Roman also breeds exotic birds – not everyone can boast of having flamingoes in their garden! Roman had bred and shown Poodles for ten years before buying his first Yorkie, from Astolat and Stirkean lines, in 1969.

Roman studied English catalogues, photographs and books, and he decided that he wanted the lovely colours of the Johnstounburn and Whitecross lines. In 1974 he bought Kingsmere Buttons, three years old and unshown – and so he had never been crackered. However, he had a long silky coat, with a glorious tan. One of his ancestors was Ch. Pagnell Peter Pan, and there was also Whitecross and Johnstounburn in the background. Within three weeks Buttons won a CC; he went on to become an International Champion, and so the Highclass line began. Roman is very knowledgeable about the breed and helped me tremendously with research for this book. He has continued on from those early days, always seeking to improve his stock but staying as close to the English lines as possible. In 1977 he bought a bitch from Betty Whitbread (Brybett), and before this bitch was exported to Germany she was mated to Ch. Blairsville Royal Seal. This mating produced Ch. Highclass Royal Seal. Roman has also worked closely with Margaret Howes of the Johnstounburn line, and has bought stock from her in order to improve his own line. Their most famous Yorkie is Int. Ch. Highclass Royal Magic Moment, a beautiful bitch who excels in both colours. She has won fifty-three CCs and is the kennel's nineteenth Champion.

KRYSTLE-LINES, Spain. Mrs Kristin Maloe founded her Yorkie kennels on stock from the Ozmilion and Eburacum lines. She lives in the centre of Madrid, and she has a small select kennel. Among her Champions is Ch. Ozmilion Millionaire, who is very typical of the Yorkies from the Ozmilion line, with a lovely head and expression and correct colours.

World Ch. My Precious Keep-Up (Belgium). (Turyanne Shannon of Shamrock – My Precious Guitar Girl). Bred and owned by Ronny and Maria Engelen.

Of MILLMOOR, MY PRECIOUS, Belgium. It was in 1966 that Ronny and Maria Engelen visited Britain in order to attend Crufts, as they had decided they would like to breed Yorkshire Terriers. Ch. My Precious Joss won the CC that year, and Ronny and Maria, who had studied books and pedigrees, had already decided that they wanted Yorkies with the Johnstounburn and Invincia bloodlines. They met Mr and Mrs Harrower of the Reworrah kennels and were able to purchase four puppies all sired by Ch. My Precious Joss. During the following two years more puppies were purchased from the Harrowers, and so the Of Millmoor kennel was founded. Both Ronny and Maria are perfectionists in all aspects of their kennel management, and I am sure that this has contributed to their outstanding success in the world of Yorkshire Terriers.

In 1973 Maria registered the prefix My Precious, in her own name, as a tribute to Ch. My Precious Joss. The most famous of the Of Millmoor Yorkies is Int. Ch. Ever Trouble Of Millmoor, who is featured on the back cover of this book. This Yorkie has influenced the breed tremendously, producing many Champions both for his breeders and for others throughout the world, particularly in Europe and North America.

RYANS HOME, SAMOTHRACE, Holland. This is an established Yorkshire Terrier kennel in Holland, owned by Messrs J. Koevoets and Koevoets-Neef. Their Yorkies include Ch. Mychah from Ryan's Home, sired by Jettrho of Ryan's Home, who is their own breeding going back to the Millmoor line, and the dam is Rowena of Ryan's Home, who again goes back to Millmoor.

SKANDIA, Denmark. Gerda Bek has been breeding Yorkies for over twenty years and has many Champions, including, in 1991, Ch. Skandias Mo Mo and Ch. Skandias Monpetit, who are litter sisters. In Denmark the breed comes under the Joint Club, for breeds without their own club; and there are seventy-one breeds included in this at the present. The Joint Club arranges five national shows a year for these breeds; Gerda is the representative for the Yorkshire Terriers.

*Ch. McMillan of
Samothrace (Holland).
Owned by H. J.
Vermeulen.*

Donvil Karl.

*Ch. Blue Victoria of
Saint Rosahof
(Holland). (Celebration
of Anasor – Beautyful
Girl of Saint Rosahof).
Bred and owned by M.
G. Renssen-Mols.*

*Ch. Gregory of Survival
(Holland). (Ch.
Gregoire – Lady
Samantha of Survival).
Bred and owned by M.
Jansen-Resoort.*

SAINT ROSAHOF, Holland. I have found it very interesting to note that many of the Yorkie Breeders in Holland have used the Kellayly line of Mrs Gwen Kellar, going back to Nelmila Berryfield Beauty, and have successfully joined this dominant line with the Of Millmoor line of Ronny and Maria Engelen. The owner of this kennel, M. G. Renssen-Mols is no exception. Ch. Blue Victoria from Saint Rosahof is sired by Celebration of Anasor and is predominantly Millmoor and Kellayly breeding. Ch. Vanessa of Anasor was bred by Mr Cranenbroek and guided to her title by M. Renssen-Mols.

SURVIVAL, Holland. Mrs Tilly Jansen-Resoort founded this kennel, and is now secretary of the Yorkshire Terrier Club in Holland. She started breeding Yorkshire Terriers in 1980. Her Yorkie bitch, Int. Ch. Lady Lotus of Survival, is sired by her own Ch. Gregory of Survival, who is a son of the famous Int. Ch. Ever Trouble of Millmoor. On the dam's side, Lady Lotus has Kellayly breeding, which goes back to Ch. Nelmila Berryfield Beauty.

TARAJA'S HOME, Holland. J. V. Lieshout, the owner of this kennel, bred Int. Ch. Dolly From Taraja's Home, sired by Sir Douglas of Anasor (who is Millmoor and Kellayly breeding) and out of the bitch, Jane From Rijan's Home, who is also mostly Millmoor line.

TORPE TINY'S, Denmark. Annelise Eriksen is founder of this kennel and has a number of Champions. They include Ch. Torpe-Tiny's Helene, a granddaughter of Ch. Blairsville Royal Seal on the sire's side, and the dam is dominantly Millmoor breeding. Annelise has been breeding Yorkies since 1980.

Ch. Torpe-Tiny's Helene (Denmark). (Int. Ch. Mardees Royal Bond of Blairsville – Cindy). Bred and owned by Annelise Eriksen.

Chapter Five

YORKSHIRE TERRIERS WORLDWIDE

There are dedicated breeders in most countries of the world, and I often wonder just what the early breeders of the Yorkshire Terrier – the men from the coal mines – would think if they could see the popularity of this charming, diminutive breed today. While researching this book I have received letters, photos and information about the breed from all over the world, and although the Yorkshire Terrier is well established in many countries, there are still some places where there are so few Yorkies that exhibitors have to travel hundreds of miles just to compete in an Open Show, and where the breed clubs are still struggling to gain recognition from their National Club. In South Africa, for instance, the Yorkie is a very popular pet, but there are not very many people who exhibit. The show enthusiasts, based in Cape Town, Durban and the Transvaal, are rarely able to compete against each other because of the vast distances involved.

Breeders from the UK have exported Yorkies throughout the world. Many have become Champions, and, with the help of dedicated breeders, they have gone on to improve the stock of the respective countries. These include Ch. Chantmarles Infatuation, who won fifty-seven CCs for his new owners in New Zealand, and the Deebees Champions, who have gone to Dr Nishi in Japan, and have also been the foundation stock of kennels throughout the world. Mrs Millard of the Nelmila Kennel has Champions in Canada and in Australia, and Mr Osman Sameja has exported his Ozmilion line to many countries. Brybett Happy Leo became a Champion in Brazil for his new owner Lacy G. Houra – and there are many more, just too numerous to mention. It is essential when exporting Yorkies that British breeders try to provide the best quality that they can, as not only will these Yorkies be ambassadors of all the Yorkies in Britain, but they are also ensuring that the future of the Yorkie in their new country is based on good sound stock.

ANCROWNES, Australia. Mrs Crosby-Brown from Sydney has been breeding Yorkies for many years, starting with stock from Barntoys which went back to Ch. Tayfirs Firegift and Buranthea lines. Probably her most successful Yorkie is Ch. Ancrownes Music Man, who is a multi Best in Show winner and also a top producer. His sire includes Macstrouds and Stirkean breeding, and the dam is Blairsville Sweet Melody. Ch. Ancrownes McPickle goes back to Barntoys and Yadnum breeding, and also to Tayfirs Firegift.

Ch. Danaliz Midnight Mist, aged fourteen months (Australia). (Ch. Ancrownes Barnaby Rudge – Terryhill Thisbie). Bred and owned by Elizabeth Shaw.

DANALIZ, Australia. Elizabeth Shaw first started breeding in Scotland in 1965, where her prefix was Danmarette. When she emigrated to Australia in 1976 she then took the prefix Danaliz, and her stock include the Blairsville and Nelmila lines. The Champion Danaliz Midnight Mist is sired by Ancrownes Barnaby Rudge and the dam is Terryhill Thisbie.

DESIDERIA, Australia. Mrs Berni Brearley started breeding Yorkies in 1963 with stock which included the Johnstounburn, Invincia, Of Wiske and the Yadnum lines. In 1980 she purchased two bitches from the Blairsville Kennels – one was a daughter of Ch. Blairsville Royal Seal, and the other was a daughter of Blairsville Royal Monarch. A son of Blairsville Royal Seal was also purchased at a later date, and these Yorkies have produced many winners for their owner.

KONIG, Selangor, West Malaysia. This kennel was founded by Mrs Caroline Ong, from Evenwood, Harleta and Ozmilion lines. Caroline only breeds when she can assure all her puppies a home with either family or friends. One of her best-known Yorkies is Ch. Nedlik Tiny Terror, who is out of My Candy Girl and sired by Happy Go Lucky at Evenwood. The heat and high humidity in Malaysia are very hard on the Yorkie coat, especially the blue, and show Yorkies must be kept in the house, out of the sun and heat.

Ch. Desideria Rose So Royal (Australia). (Balbardie My Precious – Daleas Gypsy Rose). Bred and owned by Berni Brearley.

*Ch. Brybett Happy Leo
(Brazil). Bred by Betty
Whitbread. Imported
from the UK and owned
by Iacy G. Houra.*

*Ch. Teo of Coramonte
(Japan). Bred by Jesus
Montero, imported from
Spain.*

Rafa.

REWORRAH, Australia. This kennel originated in Scotland and was founded by Mr and Mrs Harrower; it is now situated in Melbourne. Before the Harrowers emigrated some years ago, they sold puppies sired by Ch. My Precious Joss to Ronnie and Maria Engelen to form the foundation of the famous Of Millmoor kennels. Once in Australia they dominated the show scene for a number of years. Their Champions include Ch. Reworrah Glowboy, whose ancestors include Ch. My Precious Joss and the Yadnum line, Ch. Reworrah Metric, and Ch. Reworrah Sonometric.

RODSAN, Malaysia. Dr Loo Voon San started breeding Yorkies when his daughter was given a bitch as a birthday present, just for a pet. This began a love of the Yorkie breed, and another Yorkie – Ancrownes Dikham, sired by Ancrownes Fidelity – was imported from Australia. Dr Loo was helped by his sister Madam Loo Siat Lee, who does all the grooming, and Dikham became a Malaysian Champion.

Ch. Debees My Fascination (Japan). (Deebees Dancing Dan – Ch. Wellshim Madam of Deebees. Bred by Mrs D. Beech. Imported from the UK and owned by Dr and Mrs S. Nishi.

Ch. Chevawn Special Engagement at Wenwytes (Japan). (Chevawn Special Charmer – Sharisa Missys Madam). Bred by Janet Campion. Imported from the UK and owned by Dr and Mrs S. Nishi.

SANWORON, Australia. T. and S. Dealey are renowned for the excellent presentation of their Yorkies in the ring. Their top winning dogs include Ch. Ancrownes Music Man, Ch. Sanworon Wish Come True, and Ch. Sanworon Miracle Girl, using mostly the Ancrownes line, bred from the Blairsville imports.

SILKYRAINS, Japan. Dr and Mrs Nishi are very familiar with the UK show scene, as they spend nearly six months of the year at their home in London. They also travel the world, attending dog shows. They have been breeding Yorkies since 1967, and the Silkyrains Yorkies were founded mainly on the Deebees line in the early days, with Ch. Deebees Cornish Echo, Ch. Deebees Speculation and Ch. Deebees My Fascination. Later came Ch. Macstroud Soldier Blue and Macstrouds Fine-N-Dandy. Ch. Chevawn Special Engagement at Wenwytes is also with Dr and Mrs Nishi. This is quite an impressive line-up for any kennel, and added to these are Yorkies

Ch. Mactroud's Soldier Blue (Japan). (Int. Ch. Macstroud's Noble Lad – Macstroud's Society Gir). Bred by David Stroud. Imported from the UK and owned by Dr and Mrs S. Nishi.

Ch. Ancrownes Dikham (Malaysia). (Ancrownes Fidelity – Sharntarles Justine). Bred by Mrs D. Crosby-Browne. Imported from Australia and owned by M. Tan.

Ch. Chantmarles Infatuation (New Zealand). Bred by Mary Hayes and imported from the UK.

Ch. Stragar Justajule (Ch. Stragar Peter Pan – Reworrah Twitta) and Stragar Clovis (Ch. Stragar Peter Pan – Pomereens Miss Mary). (Australia).

from the Kellayly and Peglea kennels. Understandably, all these Yorkies have become Champions in Japan, and the Nishis have guided over twenty to their title, along with their other much-loved breed, the Maltese. Mrs Nishi is the secretary of the Yokohama Int. Yorkshire Terrier Club and Dr Nishi is the chairman. This club was founded in 1976.

STRAGAR, Australia. Mrs M. Hole of Melbourne imported Yorkies from the Nelmila kennel (including Nelmila Silver Lariot, son of Ch. Nelmila Berryfield Beauty), Dundry and later the Wykebank and Typros lines, in order to improve her stock. She also combined the Reworrah and Ancrownes lines to produce some top Yorkies.

TANTEEN, Australia. Mrs Suzette Woodruffe, who owns this kennel, is very aware of the tremendous difficulty that Australian breeders have in producing quality Yorkies because of the very small gene pool that is available to them. As a hobby she keeps comprehensive computer records of as many Yorkies as possible, which must be a help to all the breeders in this country. For her own show stock, she used a combination of the Blairsville and Reworrah imports, and more recently she has used the New Zealand imports from the Chantmarles and Deebees lines, including Ch. Pepa Blue Bonnet (who is a granddaughter of Ch. Ancrownes Music Man on the sire's side; the dam is Reworrah Huggy, going back to Nelmila Silver Lariot, who is a son of Ch. Nelmila Berryfield Beauty, both owned and bred by Mrs Ivy Millard), Ch. Tanteen Golden Pippin, and Ch. Tanteen Never Say Die, a son of Pippin.

VIHOVEN, South Africa. This kennel is owned by Mr Dave Keytel and is one of the foremost kennels in South Africa. He owns the top winning Yorkie for 1990 and 1991.

Chapter Six

THE BREED STANDARD

THE BRITISH BREED STANDARD

GENERAL APPEARANCE Long-coated, coat hanging quite straight and evenly down each side, a parting extending from nose to end of tail. Very compact and neat, carriage very upright conveying an important air. General outline conveying impression of vigorous and well-proportioned body.

CHARACTERISTICS Alert, intelligent toy terrier.

TEMPERAMENT Spirited with an even disposition.

HEAD AND SKULL Rather small and flat, not too prominent or round in skull, nor too long in muzzle, black nose.

EYES Medium, dark, sparkling, with sharp intelligent expression and placed to look directly forward. Not prominent. Edge of eyelids dark.

EARS Small, V-shaped, carried erect, not too far apart, covered with short hair, colour very deep, rich tan.

MOUTH Perfect, regular and complete scissor bite, i.e. the upper teeth closely overlapping the lower teeth and set square to the jaws. Teeth well placed with even jaws.

NECK Good reach.

FOREQUARTERS Well laid shoulders, legs straight, well covered with hair of rich, golden tan a few shades lighter at the ends than at the roots, not extending higher on forelegs than elbow.

BODY Compact with moderate spring of rib, good loin. Level back.

HINDQUARTERS Legs quite straight when viewed from behind, moderate turn of stifle. Well covered with hair of rich, golden tan a few shades lighter at ends than at roots, not extending higher on hindlegs than stifle.

FEET Round; nails black.

TAIL Customarily docked to medium length with plenty of hair, darker blue in colour than rest of body, especially at the end of tail. Carried a little higher than level of back.

GAIT/MOVEMENT Free with drive; straight action front and behind, retaining level topline.

COAT Hair on body moderately long, perfectly straight (not wavy), glossy, fine silky texture, not woolly. Fall on head long, rich golden tan, deeper in colour at sides of head, about ear roots and on muzzle where it should be very long. Tan on head not to extend on to neck, nor must any sooty or dark hair intermingle with any of tan.

COLOUR Dark steel blue (not silver blue), extending from occiput to root of tail, never mingled with fawn, bronze or dark hairs. Hair on chest rich, bright tan. All tan hair darker at the roots than in middle, shading to still lighter at tips.

SIZE Weight up to 3.1kgs (7lbs).

FAULTS Any departure from the foregoing points should be considered a fault and the seriousness with which the fault should be regarded should be in exact proportion to its degree.

NOTE Male animals should have two apparently normal testicles fully descended into the scrotum.

Reproduced by kind permission of the English Kennel Club.

The above is the breed standard as set down by The Kennel Club, London, England; the FCI Breed Standard is very similar. It is interesting to note the value of points, as compiled by the Yorkshire Terrier Club in 1946:

Formation and terrier appearance: 15
Colour of hair on body: 15
Richness of tan on head and legs: 15
Quality and texture of coat: 10
Quality and length of coat: 10
Head: 10

Mouth: 5
Legs and feet: 5
Ears: 5
Eyes: 5
Tail (carriage of): 5

THE AMERICAN BREED STANDARD

GENERAL APPEARANCE That of a long-haired toy terrier whose blue and tan coat is parted on the face and from the base of the skull to the end of the tail and hangs evenly and quite straight down each side of the body. The body is neat, compact and well proportioned. The dog's high head carriage and confident manner should give the appearance of vigor and self-importance.

HEAD Small and rather flat on top, the skull not too prominent or round, the muzzle not too long, with the bite neither undershot or overshot and teeth sound. Either scissors bite or level bite is acceptable. The nose is black. Eyes are medium in size and not too prominent; dark in colour and sparkling with a sharp intelligent expression. Eye rims are dark. Ears are small, V-shaped, carried erect and set not too far apart.

BODY Well proportioned and very compact. The back is rather short, the back line level, with height at shoulder the same as at the rump.

LEGS AND FEET Forelegs should be straight, elbows neither in nor out. Hindlegs straight when viewed from behind, but stifles are moderately bent when viewed from the sides. Feet are round with black toenails. Dewclaws, if any, are generally removed from the hind legs. Dewclaws on the forelegs may be removed.

TAIL Docked to a medium length and carried slightly higher than the level of the back.

COAT Quality, texture and quantity of coat are of prime importance. Hair is glossy, fine and silky in texture. Coat on the body is moderately long and perfectly straight (not wavy). It may be trimmed to floor length to give ease of movement and a neater appearance, if desired. The fall on the head is long, tied with one bow in center of head or parted in the middle and tied with two bows. Hair on muzzle is very long. Hair should be trimmed short on tips of ears and may be trimmed on feet to give them a neat appearance.

COLORS Puppies are born black and tan and are normally darker in body color, showing an intermingling of black hair in the tan until they are matured. Color of hair on body and richness of tan on head and legs are of prime importance in adult dogs to which the following color requirements apply:
BLUE: is a dark steel-blue, not a silver-blue and not mingled with fawn, bronzy or black hairs.
TAN: All tan hair is darker at the roots than in the middle, shading to still lighter tan at the tips. There should be no sooty or black hair intermingled with any of the tan.

COLOR ON BODY The blue extends over the body from back of neck to root of tail. Hair on tail is a darker blue, especially at end of tail.

HEADFALL A rich golden tan, deeper in color at sides of head, at ear roots and on the muzzle, with ears a deep rich tan. Tan color should not extend down on back of neck.

CHEST AND LEGS A bright rich tan, not extending above the elbow on the forelegs nor above the stifle on the hindlegs.

WEIGHT Must not exceed seven pounds.

Reproduced by kind permission of the American Kennel Club.

INTERPRETING THE BREED STANDARD

The differences between the British and American Breed Standards are very little. The American Standard does mention the colour of puppies, which is excellent, as the puppies in our breed are so different from the adults. The British Standard does not mention the ribbon on the head, which I think is just as well, as it is only an embellishment to the head, and is not part of the dog. It is very healthy for our breed that the Breed Standards are basically the same; I hope that it always stays this way. For clarity, I will refer to them as one Standard, mentioning any main differences that occur. The Breed Standard is the guide that we use to compare our dogs with, whether we are judging, breeding, showing, or wanting to know whether our pet is typical of the breed. This Standard can be interpreted in several ways; however, the following interpretation is the one I consider the most widely accepted, both by renowned breeders and very experienced judges worldwide. It is important to remember that the Standard refers to a mature, adult Yorkie.

CHARACTERISTICS
The characteristics of a Yorkie are described as being those of an "alert, intelligent toy terrier". It is worth analysing this description word by word:
ALERT: This is the understatement of the day. Yorkies never miss a thing, whether guarding a house or minding someone else's business – they are right there in the thick of it.
INTELLIGENT: This is undeniable; sometimes it would be easier if they were not quite so intelligent!
TOY: I think we should always be very conscious of this word; toy is what they are, and toy is what they should be. In a number of countries now, they have been transferred to the Terrier Group, which is, in my opinion, a great pity. I often hear breeders from overseas saying: "The Yorkie has to be larger now to be in contention with so many larger breeds; after all, it is a Terrier." This, to me, is an incorrect statement, and I think that most, if not all breeders in Britain would agree with me. The Yorkshire Terrier is a *toy terrier;* it complements the other toy breeds such as the dainty Papillon and the glamorous Maltese. Did our early breeders strive to create and perfect this diminutive toy dog, with its unique coat and delightful disposition, only to have it 'changed' to fit the Group? I think not.

TEMPERAMENT
Temperament should be "spirited, with an even disposition, and I think this describes the Yorkie exactly. Just watch the little 'angels' on their red boxes in the show ring – butter wouldn't melt in their mouths! A Yorkie will stand patiently waiting to be seen by the judge; it will stand for a prolonged amount of time when it is being groomed, nearly falling asleep at times because it is so relaxed. But just let something arouse and threaten this 'paragon', perhaps another dog or something it considers threatening to its owner, and watch this little 'angel' turn into a ferocious

Ch. Ozmilion Dedication (UK) showing his overall balance and outstanding quality. (Ch. Ozmilion Admiration – Ch. Ozmilion Hearts Desire). Bred and owned by Osman Sameja.

Thomas Fall.

Ch. Blairsville Royal Seal (UK) with his alert expression and faultless topline. (Ch. Beechrise Surprise – Ch. Blairsville Most Royale). Bred and owned by Mr and Mrs B. Lister.

defender, with little or no thought for its own size, or lack of it. A Yorkie will take on the world at times, with absolutely no hope of winning – that is the type of dog it is, fearless to the end.

One of my own Yorkies, Sasha, a Brybett bitch, considered herself defender of everything that was mine, particularly what she considered was my chair. She didn't like other people to sit in the chair, she certainly would not allow other dogs near it, although she did relax this rule for herself! One day our Rottweiler bitch, Marni, sat a little too close to the chair, so Sasha warned her off. Marni, knowing that the little Yorkie was the 'boss' and not to be trifled with, moved what could have only been an inch. Again Sasha warned her, and again Marni moved another inch. This went on until Sasha was quite beside herself – she was so angry – and Marni was getting bored with the whole procedure, but still moving inch by inch towards the door, with Sasha dancing round her. Finally Marni must have decided that enough was enough and went outside to play. Immediately, Sasha ran and hid behind the door and wouldn't move. I watched with fascination; she was obviously up to something, but what, I couldn't imagine. Then all became clear when Marni eventually returned – Sasha flew at her from behind the door and swung on Marni's throat. Marni stood stock-still in shock and disbelief. At this juncture I shouted at Sasha to let the Rottweiler go. She immediately loosened her hold and dropped to the floor. Marni looked down at her with a puzzled expression, but she had got the message and turned on her heels and left again. Sasha was triumphant; she had established beyond any doubt that she, not Marni, was boss and Marni must do as she was told. This story is typical of a Yorkie, and all Yorkie owners will be able to recall similar incidents. A Yorkie is completely fearless when it comes to defending what it feels is right, even if sometimes it is a little misguided. It also speaks volumes for the temperament of the Rottweiler: a dear soul who adored our Yorkies, she was one of Judy and Larry Elsden's Chesera breeding, a 'Royal' in her own right.

HEAD
The Yorkie head should appear small in comparison to its body. If the head is large it tends to look more like an Australian Silky Terrier, and the petite face and features are completely lost. The skull must be flat and not rounded, with the eyes set to look forward, not set on the side. The muzzle should not be too long – but not so short that the Yorkie resembles one of the short-nosed breeds such as a Pekingese.

EYES
The eyes must have black rims, often referred to as 'mascara'; without these black rims the dog appears to have a 'piggy' expression. The eyes should not bulge; they should be dark, sparkling, and full of fun, with an expression of intelligence. Light eyes spoil this expression, and are most undesirable.

NOSE
The nose must be black; brown or pale noses are considered a bad fault in the breed. Fortunately this is not a prevalent fault in Yorkies, and I think that any dog that has this defect should not be exhibited in the show ring.

EARS
The ears should be small and V-shaped, set not too wide apart, in balance with the head. They

Correct ear-set.

Semi-erect ears.

Dropped ears.

Ears too large and too wide set.

Ch. Clantalon Contention (UK) illustrating a balanced head, with correct-shaped ears and small, well-placed eyes. (Meadpark Personality Plus – Nelmila Berryfield Opal).
Bred and owned by Mr and Mrs Douglas McKay.

should not be so large that they flop, although the floppy ears are more often seen in the larger type Yorkie. On the other hand, the ears should not be so small that they look ridiculous in comparison to the head. Ears that are set wide apart towards the side of the head always appear to me to give a Yorkie a comical expression, and so that alert expression, so desired, is lost.

MOUTH
A Yorkie mouth should have a perfect scissor bite, with a full complement of teeth. It should be neither undershot (bottom jaw and teeth protruding in front of the top jaw and teeth), nor overshot (top jaw and teeth protruding in front of the bottom jaw and teeth, leaving a gap between). A wry mouth (jaws and teeth both crooked) is also very undesirable. On the whole, bad mouths are not prevalent in the breed, although if we relax our vigilance, they could easily become so, as with other toy breeds.

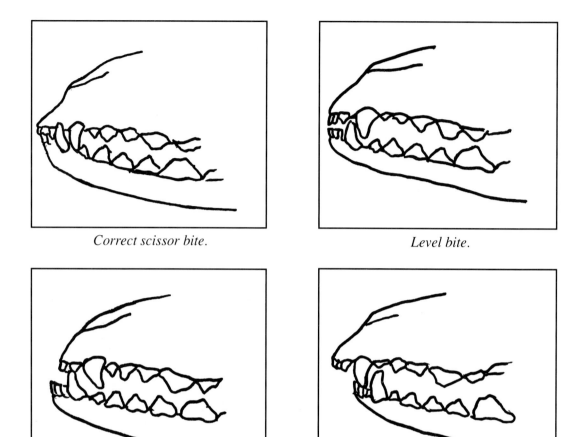

Correct scissor bite.   *Level bite.*

Undershot.   *Overshot.*

NECK

The reach of neck is something that I could really wax lyrical about! I believe that a good reach of neck is essential as it gives the Yorkie that 'important air', that upright carriage, and the extra elegance. I have yet to see a Yorkie with hardly any neck possess any of these attributes.

BODY

The neck should be set in to well-laid shoulders and lead to a completely level topline. A level topline is a 'must' for a Yorkie. Far too often we see Yorkies dipping behind the shoulders, or with roach backs, and these Yorkies will never be able to move correctly. A dog that is not built correctly will never be able to move correctly. The body should be compact with a moderate spring of rib. A number of Yorkies are too narrow all through, and so they do not have this spring of rib, resulting in a number of faults, and possible complications when whelping.

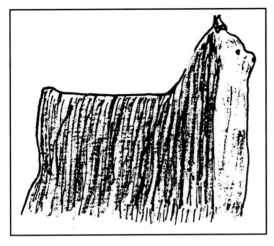

Correct.

Tail carriage too high.

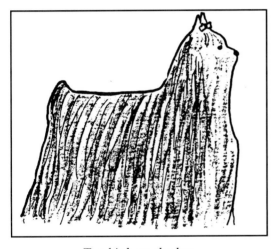

Too high on the leg.

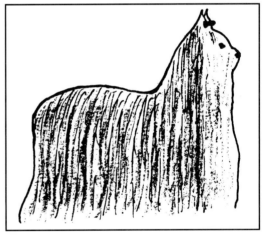

Roach back.

FOREQUARTERS
The forelegs should be quite straight when viewed from the front and the side. When viewed from the side, the feet should be in a straight line under the point of the shoulder blades, at the withers.

HINDQUARTERS
The hindlegs should be straight when viewed from behind, and with a moderate turn of stifle when viewed from the side. There should be no exaggeration either way; too straight a stifle is often a pointer to an unsound joint, as is too much turn of stifle (resembling the stifle of a German Shepherd Dog).

FEET

The foot should be round, somewhat similar to cats' feet. Feet that are long (hare-like) are undesirable, although I have to add that incorrect shaped feet are not prevalent in the breed. A more common fault is feet that turn outwards, when viewed from the side. The nails should be black in colour. White nails signify a lack of pigmentation, and may be a pointer to lack of pigmentation around the eyes and in the coat colour.

TAIL

It states very clearly in the Breed Standard that the tail should be carried a little higher than the back. This does not mean straight up like a flag, either on the show box or on the move. I am fully aware that this can look very smart, and that it tends to shorten the look of the back – not that any judge worth their salt is going to be fooled by that. In America the custom is to pose the dog with its tail held up. In Europe some exhibitors tend to push the head so far back and the tail so far forward, that it distorts the outline. I also think it must be very uncomfortable for the dog.

MOVEMENT

On the move, the Yorkie should be a joy to behold, driving from the hindquarters and covering the ground with great purpose, not ambling or mincing or appearing to pick its way over uneven ground, but really moving, with level topline and that 'important air'. The Yorkie is a busy dog; it always has somewhere to go. A Yorkie who is really moving always reminds me of the song from the musical version of *Alice in Wonderland*: "I'm late, I'm late, for a very important date, no time to say hello, goodbye, I'm late, I'm late, I'm late."

COAT AND COLOUR

The coat of the Yorkie is its dominant feature, with its beautiful colours of dark steel-blue and rich, golden tan, set on silk. It takes so long to grow and nurture this coat – with the colours continually changing throughout the Yorkie's life. This is perhaps what makes this most prized of coats so fascinating. It always brings a lump to my throat to see a Yorkie in full, flowing coat moving across the grass in the summer sunshine – but it is also what makes the Yorkie so very difficult to judge. In an attempt to simplify the intricacies of this dark steel-blue coat, I have categorised the different textures. I do not pretend that all the textures fit into these categories, but the majority either fit or come between them.

Ch. Status Quo at Beechrise (UK) demonstrating correct movement, Crufts 1992. (Ch. Ozmilion Admiration – Rozamie Emotional Desire). Bred by Joe Magri. Owned by Mrs Hilda Griffiths.

Int. Ch. Bajazzo's Mandy (Germany) showing tremendous length of falls. (Highclass Merry Mark – Highclass Tutti-Frutti). Bred and owned by Rudi and Wally Hodl.

THE DARK, STEEL-BLUE, SILK COAT: This is the correct coat that we all strive for. It must extend from the occiput to the root of the tail, being darker on the tail. Try to imagine a piece of silk material: its texture is fine, but it has a certain hardness about it, and the true Yorkie coat is the same. The dark, steel-blue colour has been likened to polished steel, and it should be completely even in colour. It must never be silver-blue. The silver-blue coats tend to wave, and they are softer to the touch. There are more arguments concerning textures of coats than anything else in our breed, although it is strange that we all agree when a true, silk coat appears.

THE SILVER-BLUE COAT: With a silver-blue coat, the colour changes at a very early age; sometimes puppies are totally changed in colour by the time that they are six months old. Unfortunately, by the time they are twelve months old or so, the steel-blue is silver, which is very upsetting for the owner. However, in some lines this light-blue can hold or even darken a little. The coat feels slightly soft to the touch, and is often wavy.

THE COTTON COAT: This coat feels exactly as though cotton-wool has been combed out. The coat is dark and lacks lustre, but it is not thick or woolly. It is fine and can be groomed absolutely straight. To the untrained eye, it will appear very dark blue in colour; in actual fact it is slate-colour. This coat is not correct and should be avoided.

THE HARSH COAT: This is a texture that is easily recognizable in an adult, simply because as it grows it breaks off and never gets to any length, and it is harsh to the touch. It is not so easy to

Int. Ch. M'Nishi of Millmoor (Belgium). A superb study of handling and presentation by Norberte De Cleen. (Ch. My Precious Joss 11 – Getback Of Millmoor). Bred and owned by Ronny and Maria Engelen.

detect in a puppy, as the coat is slow-growing like a true silk. By the time the puppy is six months old it will be sparse, and it will not be growing evenly, as though it has been broken or damaged. The colour normally remains black. This coat is not correct and should be avoided.

THE BLACK, WOOLLY COAT: It is not a coincidence that I have left this texture of coat until last. Ask any breeder what they think of a 'black woolly' and they will throw up their hands in horror! This is the worst texture coat that a Yorkie can have, and very much to be avoided. It is very fast-growing and very thick. It is very soft, like wool, to the touch, and appears somewhat frizzy on the ends. Puppies look as though they have a frill. The coat completely lacks lustre; but beware, would-be judges – the 'black woolly' often appears very glamorous, particularly when it is coupled with excellent structure and movement. This type is often lacking neck, but frequently has the face of an angel. How many times have we seen judges taken in by the glamour of this type?

TAN MARKINGS: The tan on the head should be a beautiful, clear gold; it has been likened to a wedding ring in colour. It should be slightly darker on the sides, on the ears and the muzzle. The tan should be darker at the roots, shading out to the lightest at the tips. Lack of this shading – when the tan is all one colour – is called a 'block tan', and does harden the expression. The tan should never 'run' into the blue anywhere, neither on the neck, above the elbows on the forelegs, above the stifle on the hind legs, or on the tail. It is important to consider the age of the dog when assessing the clear, golden tan on the head. A youngster will not have this colour; it comes with maturity. This is the reason why most Yorkie specialists do not like to see a puppy receive CCs in the show ring, as it cannot truly conform to the Breed Standard.

The challenge of attempting to breed and show a Yorkie, which matures physically at the same point that the coat and colour reach maturity, is tremendous. Add to this the requirements of correct coat colour and texture, and correct overall structure, and it is easy to see why the Yorkie is such a difficult dog to breed and judge. Of course, we all breed and exhibit the dog that comes closest to the Breed Standard, and it is healthy for the breed that we attend shows and compare our dogs with others in the ring. This is the best way of learning about other lines, and trying to improve our dogs. No one is infallible, and we all take a retrograde step at times with our breeding, for no matter how hard we study the pedigrees and the dogs, nature has the last word. All breeders have a great responsibility as keepers of the breed: we do not own it, we are only able to look after it and try to improve it during our lifetime. The legacy that we leave for future generations should be that the Yorkshire Terrier is the delightful toy terrier (although, hopefully, improved upon) that we inherited from breeders well over a hundred years ago.

Chapter Seven

THE COMPANION YORKIE

I make no apologies for dedicating this chapter to the first-time owner – the person who is a newcomer to this delightful breed. I have tried to answer some of the questions that I have been asked over the years, and, indeed, the questions that I asked when I was a first-time owner, as we all have been. I hope that this chapter will be helpful to novices, so that they can enjoy their Yorkies to the full. To the people who already own Yorkies and know most if not all the information contained here, I invite you to read this chapter through; it will bring back memories of when you had your first Yorkie, and how even the simplest task appeared very complicated. Even while writing, it made me think, once again, how very patient we should be with our new owners.

IS THE YORKSHIRE TERRIER THE BREED FOR YOU?

Before embarking on buying your first Yorkie, there are many points to consider. This bundle of fun is hopefully going to be a member of your family for a very long time, so it is important to ensure that this is the breed for you and your family, and will suit your lifestyle. The Yorkshire Terrier is a comparatively young breed, and it has been bred down in size in a short space of time. It therefore stands to reason that size differs far more than the weight (of up to seven pounds) stipulated by the Breed Standard. I would never recommend that a family with young children buys a Yorkie which will be very tiny when it becomes an adult. This sort of family would be far better suited to a larger type of Yorkie, who will love to play with the children and go for long walks. On the other hand, if you live alone or there are only adults in the family, then a tiny Yorkie could be ideal.

The character of the Yorkie is delightful: it is a very intelligent, fun-loving dog, and it is always busy. It is a typical terrier, which surprises a lot of people, who tend to think of the Yorkie as a lap dog. When people have come to buy one of our puppies, nine times out of ten the husband will declare that he would never be seen dead with "that" on the end of a lead. Several weeks later, when they come to visit with their Yorkie, it is always the husband who boasts how intelligent the puppy is, and is the first to describe all the little idiosyncrasies of its character. The so-called 'lap dog' will be happy and content to sit by you for as long as you sit, but it rarely

The Yorkie is an intelligent, fun-loving dog.

By kind permission of the Y.T.C. Re-homing Scheme

enjoys actually being on your lap; and if it is a lap dog that you want, then I feel that you would be better advised to buy another breed. Yorkies live quite happily in a town flat, and will content themselves equally well in a small space as on a country estate, where they can romp across the fields. They adjust well to most types of environment, and, of course, the Yorkie does not shed its coat, so there are no problems with dog hairs spoiling your best carpets and furniture.

One of the decisions to be made when buying a puppy is whether you would prefer a dog or a bitch. Unlike the larger breeds, there is little difference in temperament, both are equally loving, so it is a matter of personal preference. What must be taken into consideration is that if you have a bitch she will come into season every six months, and will have to be watched very closely during this time.

BUYING A YORKIE

When you are confident that a Yorkie is the breed for you, the next step is to find a reputable breeder. If you are a newcomer to the breed, the best starting point is the national Kennel Club, and then you will be able to obtain the name and address of the nearest Breed Club Secretary, who will be able to help you with names and addresses of reputable breeders. When you make contact with a breeder, try to give some idea of your lifestyle, the size of your family, and the ages of your children (if any). The breeder will want to know if someone is in the house for most of the day, as a young puppy cannot be left alone for long periods. All this information will help the breeder work out what type of puppy will suit you. Time spent at this stage is a good investment, for both you and the puppy.

Having ascertained that the breeder has a puppy that might suit your family, arrangements should be made to view the litter. Early afternoon is a sensible time to visit the kennels, so that if you purchase the puppy and take it home, it will have time to settle down and accustom itself a little to its new surroundings before going to bed for the night. The breeder should show you the parents of the puppies, or at least the mother, and this will give you some idea as to the size the pup will grow to, and its temperament. Puppies are always enchanting, but try to curb your enthusiasm, and just sit quietly and watch their antics. When a litter is left to its own devices, the puppies will soon start to show their true characters, and soon, I am sure, you will be drawn to one particular puppy. It might be the most inquisitive, the busiest, or even the bossiest. While you are sitting watching the puppies, note their general demeanour. Are they happy, playful, bright and clear-eyed? After a few minutes, kneel on the floor with the puppies. Never attempt to pick up a pup until invited to do so by the breeder. Young puppies can soon wriggle out of your hands, and accidents happen very quickly, so it is better to get down with the puppies, and the pups themselves seem to prefer it.

It is a good idea to note down a list of questions to ask the breeder. It is easy to get so captivated by the puppies that you forget to ask the most obvious questions. For instance:

1. What date was the puppy born?
2. Is it registered with the national Kennel Club?
3. Has it had any inoculations? If not, when are they due?
4. How many meals a day does it eat, and at what time?
5. What food does it eat?
6. Does it drink milk? (Milk does not suit a lot of Yorkies.)

Obviously you will have your own questions to add to this list. In most instances the breeder will supply a diet sheet for the puppy, and I think it is important not to change the diet for some time, until you are confident that the puppy has settled into its new home.

ARRIVING HOME

The puppy's first few days in its new home can be very stressful, and it is important that you give it all possible consideration at this time. It is probably the first time it has been separated from its mother and its brothers and sisters, and it is likely to feel very frightened as everything is so strange. I often wish that I could explain to a puppy everything that is going to happen to it in its new home. Instead, you, as its new family, must show as much love and consideration as you can. One small word of warning: a Yorkshire puppy may be only ten weeks old or so when it comes into its new home, but it is very clever and will take advantage of any situation. It is therefore important that you do not allow bad habits to develop, as they will be very hard to eliminate as the puppy gets older. This problem can arise much more quickly than you would imagine, and habits which appeared amusing in a ten-week-old puppy can be downright aggravating in an adult.

Yorkies are also very quick at sizing up situations, as I learnt very quickly with my first Craigsbank Yorkie, who was known as Pippa. An elderly lady used to visit us, and she would make a bee-line for Pippa as soon as she came into the house. Unfortunately, she was one of the

Konig Satin Lady (Malaysia), bred and owned by Caroline Ong. A new puppy arriving home has a lot of new things to get used to.

The best bed for a new puppy is a cardboard box, but Ch. Tiffany's Dixie Charmer (USA), bred by Beverly Ferguson and Catherine Sheridan, owned by Dolores Densten, shows that all Yorkies enjoy a life of luxury.

brigade that believes that Yorkies are lap dogs, so she would always pick up Pippa, and hold her firmly in her lap, until Pippa squirmed to get free. After a number of visits, Pippa only had to hear the lady's voice, and she would run for cover under one of the chairs, only coming out to disgrace herself on the carpet, in front of the lady. Obviously, she was horrified that we allowed such a "dirty" dog in our sitting-room, and I couldn't explain that Pippa was doing it on purpose. However, as far as Pippa was concerned, it did the trick, and the lady never attempted to pick her up again – the smug expression on that dog's face was unbelievable!

The best bed for the puppy for the first few months is a fairly small cardboard box with a blanket in it, placed in a draught-free corner of the kitchen and surrounded with newspaper. When the puppy is ten weeks old it should still be sleeping for most of the day, only playing for twenty minutes or so between meals. If your house is very busy with lots of people about, do make sure that the puppy gets its rest, as it is essential to the puppy's development and well-being. Try to stay, as far as possible, with the routine and diet prescribed by the breeder. Remember that any changes you want to make in your puppy's life should be introduced slowly, whether it is diet or general routine. A sudden change can upset a puppy's entire system and make it extremely unwell. The puppy may cry after you have put it to bed on its first night. I always think that a warm hot-water bottle under the blanket helps tremendously, and a cuddly toy to snuggle up against can also be a comfort, providing the stuffing is safe (definitely not a sponge filling) and puppy cannot chew off the eyes.

After a few days, make an appointment to take your puppy to the vet for a check-up, and to have any inoculations it may require. The inoculations are given as a course of two injections, two weeks apart. The first of these is usually administered at ten weeks, but your vet will advise you on this. If there is an epidemic of parvo virus in your area, he may want to give the puppy immunity earlier. (Details of the inoculations required are given in Chapter Fourteen: General Health Care). The first visit to the vet is important, as it allows your puppy and the vet to become acquainted while the puppy is well. Whenever we take our Yorkies out in the car we always put them in a travelling box – these are available at any good pet shop. We put a blanket in the box, and when you get to the vet you can put the blanket on the table for the puppy to sit on. This is a precaution against infection. Do not allow the puppy on the floor while you are in the surgery, and make sure you do not let it come into contact with any other dog in the waiting-room; most other animals are only there because they are sick. The vet will advise you when it will be safe to take your puppy out for a walk.

Worming is a very necessary procedure, both for the puppy's health and for the sake of general hygiene. It should be done at regular intervals of approximately every six months throughout the dog's life. Worming will not harm your puppy in any way, providing the worming medication is not too strong. Your vet can advise you on the most suitable product to use. I find that a worming cream is the easiest to use. All you have to do is squeeze the appropriate amount (following the manufacturer's instructions) on to the first finger of your right hand, gently open the puppy's mouth with your left hand, and draw the worming cream off on to the roof of the mouth. The dose must be repeated two weeks later to ensure that larvae and worms have been eradicated.

LEAD TRAINING

The next big event in your puppy's life is training it to the lead. This can be quite traumatic for the youngster, so always be very patient and set aside a few minutes each day for the task. I always find that the best way to start is to put the collar and lead on the puppy in the house, and then let it wander around, leaving the lead trailing. However, do not leave the puppy unattended, in case the lead gets caught on something. If you allow the puppy to roam, wearing its lead, for a few minutes a day, for several days, it will soon ignore the lead completely. This is the time to pick up the lead and follow the puppy around, making sure that the lead does not go taut. Then, start to call the puppy, encouraging it to follow you. Again, this may take a few days, but soon the puppy will find it fun and enjoy the mini training sessions. Give your puppy loads of praise for any step it takes. It is essential that the puppy understands that it is pleasing you, and it will soon associate this with doing what you ask. When you are training, never get irritated with your puppy. If you start feeling cross and frustrated, it is time to give up, and try again another time.

DEVELOPING YOUR PUPPY'S CHARACTER

Puppies love to play, and toys are an important part of their physical and mental development. We keep a small cardboard box especially for puppy toys: balls, rubber bones, old slippers, even ladies' tights folded and tied in the middle, are all favourite playthings. When a puppy is playing with a toy it is getting useful exercise, improving its co-ordination and its mental powers, as it tries out new games. However, do not let the puppy play for too long, so that it becomes exhausted.

Yorkies like to be wherever you are, and their small size means that they can follow you about without getting in the way. I am sure that this close association helps them to develop such a marvellous character. When I am doing the housework, never in one place for more than two minutes, Nana, my dearest friend and pet, will move from room to room, upstairs and downstairs – and she never appears to get bored. She just watches what I am doing, and, in fact, she now knows my routine as well as I do. She is always at the next job before me, waiting with her head on one side, interested, alert, and full of fun. Sometimes I vary the routine to try and fool her; this she thinks is as funny as I do – these Yorkies have a real sense of humour!

HOUSE TRAINING.

House training should be started as soon as possible. When your puppy wakes up, just pick it up and put it outside for a few minutes, until it has 'performed'. Then give it plenty of praise for being so good. This procedure should be followed after every meal, and each time it wakes up. It is important that you are totally consistent when you are house training, and give it all your attention. Yorkies love to please, and they will be quick to learn what is required. However, if you only put your puppy out a couple of times, and then forget, the puppy will become confused and not understand what you want. If you work at the task, it should only take a few days.

SOCIALISING YOUR PUPPY

Once your puppy has had all of its inoculations it is time to socialise it by going for walks, meeting your friends, and generally integrating it as a full member of your family. The more work that you put in at this juncture – if one can call it work – the more pleasure your Yorkie will give you for the rest of its life. There is nothing more enjoyable than a happy, well adjusted Yorkie, but there is nothing worse than a spoilt little brat – and believe me, they do exist, and in virtually every instance it is the owner who is at fault for not training and socialising the puppy correctly in those first formative months.

A local dog training club is a good place to socialise your Yorkie. Most clubs have meetings once a week or once a fortnight, and you will find people who are only too willing to help you and your puppy. It is also a social occasion, and your puppy will make a lot of new friends. I ran a training club for nine years, and I have seen many raw, awkward puppies grow and develop, and many novice owners, who have gained so much experience from everyone at the club. I loved to listen to the general hubbub of conversation of the owners, with their dogs beside them, just enjoying the evening; and then, when asked, the dogs would work like mad to please their owners in the training exercises.

During this period of socialisation when your puppy is getting used to many new experiences, you may find that there is something that it takes a particular dislike to, or is particularly worried about, such as cars whizzing by or loud noises. It is very important that you take time to help the puppy over its fears. A car speeding past must be terrifying for a tiny little dog, so start by picking your puppy up when approaching a busy road: talk to it quietly and hold it close to you. Take things slowly, and do not make the puppy walk until you are sure that it has stopped shaking. It needs to realise that although the cars are big and noisy, they will not hurt, as long as puppy and owner stay close together.

All dogs seem to thrive on routine, and the Yorkie is no exception; they seem to draw a lot of confidence and pleasure from knowing what time they are going to be fed, taken for a walk, or played with. They definitely have a built-in clock, so do not get fixed into too strict a routine, otherwise the dog will become demanding. The best idea is to vary the times a little, so the dog knows the routine, but you are not tied down to doing everything to order. However, I think the puppy should be fed at the same times every day. Other breeders may well disagree, but I feel that when, they are very young, puppies need to be fed on time; and adult dogs, like humans, certainly prefer to know when they can expect their next meal. Most dogs prefer a little peace and quiet at mealtimes, so make sure children are not hanging around in the kitchen and don't suddenly appear from nowhere – I know mine do, two-legged and four-legged alike, when they think food is in the offing!

CARE OF THE COAT

One of the main problems that is encountered by first-time owners of Yorkshire Terriers is how to look after the coat. In fact, this is quite easy, although I always warn would-be owners that they must spend at least a few minutes grooming their dog every day, and it must be bathed at least once a fortnight. It seems that some people regard the prospect of grooming a dog as a chore, which will not be enjoyable for dog or owner. This does not have to be the case at all. In fact, I find grooming is one of the most relaxing times in my day. When I explain my method of grooming to new owners, they very often tell me later how much they enjoy this daily care of the dog. I always choose a time in the day when the household is fairly quiet, and I make sure I have enough time available, so I will not have to rush. The grooming equipment that you require is:

A small bristle brush.
A stainless steel comb.
A fine-toothed comb.

Int. Ch. Shakespeare's Double Delight (Canada). (Shakespeare's As You Like It – Ch. Pastoral Devils Delight). Bred by Roxanne Miligan and Diane Kijowski. Owned by Anne Robert. A Yorkie's coat is its crowning glory – but it takes hard work and dedication to keep it in full coat. Alex Smith.

Cotton wool (cotton).
Eye drops (such as Optrex).
A pair of scissors (hair-dressing type).
A pair of nail-clippers.
A small steel file (about 6 ins long, as used for cars).
A spray bottle containing water.
Rubber bands or small hair clips.
A small towel.

It sounds a lot for one little body, but you will find that having everything you need in one place is a great help. I keep my grooming tools in a plastic box, but any container will do – a biscuit tin is just as good. The easiest way to groom a Yorkie is to stand it on a small table, a card table is ideal, and then you can settle yourself on a chair with the table in front of you. Put the towel on the table, and then, gently, place the puppy on the table, holding it firmly around the neck with your left hand. Never let go of the puppy while it is on the table, and, of course, never leave it unattended on the table. This sounds like commonsense, but on many occasions I have seen Yorkies left unattended at dog shows. This, I think, is unforgivable, and it is only a matter of time before an accident occurs. So do not be tempted to leave your dog alone, no matter how well-behaved it is.

The first step in the grooming routine is to pour a little Optrex (eye drops) on to a cotton ball, and gently wipe the eyes from the corner to the outside, removing any mucus or dirt that may have collected there. Make sure you use a fresh cotton ball for each eye. When puppies are around three months old the coat is at a length when it seems to be growing from the bridge of the nose into the eyes, making the eyes run, and the Optrex will help combat this. Then spray the coat with a fine mist of water, just a little is sufficient, and this will enable you to comb the coat out more easily. Starting with the face, carefully brush the hair down each side of the nose, and brush from above the eyes upwards towards the ears. Then brush under the ears in a downwards direction. Move behind the ears, and continue brushing down the back, lifting the coat occasionally to make sure the underneath is tangle-free. Do not forget to brush the legs, underneath the belly, and the chest, finishing with the rear end and tail. All this should be done slowly, talking to the puppy and soothing it. At first your puppy may try to struggle on the table, but the more calm you are, the more calm your puppy will become, until you both enjoy the grooming sessions. Once the brushing is completed, start the whole process again, this time with the steel combs. Use the small fine-toothed comb first, and, starting with the face, gently comb around the muzzle and then above the eyes towards the ears, just as you did with the brush, until you have completely combed the puppy all the way through to the skin. One of the most common mistakes made by first-time owners is failing to groom all the way through to the skin, and before they know where they are, the coat is completely matted up underneath. This is an horrendous job to deal with for the owner, but more especially for the puppy, so do be careful that you do not to fall into this trap. Lastly comes the top-knot of hair, which should be put in a rubber band or a child's hair-clip, taking care not to pull the hair too tight. The puppy will soon tell you if it is uncomfortable by trying to scratch out the band or rubbing its head on the carpet. I have never had much success with the hair-clip, the puppies just seem to shake their heads and out it comes, so I always use rubber bands – but you may have more luck!

BATHING

A puppy should be bathed every two weeks, more often if necessary. The reason for this is that Yorkies do not shed their coats, so bathing is the only way of keeping their coat, and their skin, clean. You will soon learn when your puppy needs a bath: the coat looks dull and dusty, and when you try to comb it, the comb seems to catch in the coat and it feels clogged. If you have taken your puppy into the woods or across the fields and the coat has got a little tangled, you will find it much easier to groom if you bath the puppy first. It helps if you use plenty of conditioner on the coat, and brush and comb it out while it is still wet.

Bathing a puppy for the first time can be very nerve-racking for the owner, but again, I say, be calm and gentle, and just think that each time you bath your puppy, it will become easier and more enjoyable for you both. I always bath my dogs in the sink, but you can use a bath or shower unit, whichever you find more convenient. Make sure you get everything prepared before you start bathing. You will need your grooming box, a couple of towels, a plastic beaker and a good shampoo. I always use Johnsons baby shampoo for the head, which is readily available from pharmacists, and Vetzyme J.D.S. for the body, which can be obtained from pet shops. You will need a good conditioner; I always use Silkience conditioner, which seems to suit the Yorkie's silky coat, but this is a matter of personal preference. After the bath is completed you will need to dry your puppy with a hair dryer. Again, you can use any type, but by far the easiest is one that has its own stand for a table. This leaves both hands free for holding the pup, and for grooming. If you only have a hand hair-dryer, it is very simple to make your own little stand for it.

Prepare the grooming table with all your equipment to hand, and cover it with one of the towels. I always brush the puppy through before bathing, just leaving any tangles, which are easier to manage when the coat is wet and conditioned. The golden rule is to never let go of your puppy while you are bathing it. This is best managed by holding the pup with your left hand, and working with your right hand. Place a cotton ball in each ear to prevent the water and soap going down them, and take great care when bathing the face and head to prevent the soap going in the eyes and up the nose – this could be most unpleasant for your puppy; it might make it panic. and put it off being bathed for a long time. This is one of the reasons I use baby shampoo on the head and face, as it does not sting if by any chance it gets into the eyes. The whole body should be soaped thoroughly, right down to the skin, not forgetting the chest, belly and back end. Then rinse well, and repeat the whole process. Finish by applying the conditioner, leaving it in the coat for a few minutes before rinsing. It is important to rinse thoroughly to make sure you have got all traces of shampoo and conditioner out of the coat. Then wrap the puppy in a towel, and remove as much water as you can before using the hair dryer – don't forget to take the cotton balls out of the ears. Dry the coat with the controls of the hair dryer set on medium, never hot or cold, and brush all the time that you are drying. If there are a few tangles, switch off the dryer and, using a comb, gently tease the tangles out; if the tangles are quite stubborn you may need the help of another person to hold the puppy's head. The best method of combing through a tangle is to place the thumb and index finger of the left hand firmly round the hair, *above* the tangle, which prevents your hurting the puppy, and then using the fine-toothed steel comb, gently tease the tangle out, holding the comb vertically and using short downward strokes. When you are drying your puppy make sure it is completely dry underneath, paying particular attention to under the neck and under the top of the legs. When you have completed this stage, allow the puppy to have a good run round and a little play before continuing your task. If you try to keep a pup on the table for too long when it is very young, it will become bored by the whole procedure. If you gradually increase the length of time it spends on the table, it will be content to stand for as long as you want when it is an adult, because it is enjoying the whole procedure. After the little break, it is back to the table, and just go through your daily routine of brushing and combing and tying up the top-knot. Bathtime is a good time to check nails, ears and feet.

NAILS

Clipping the nails is a task that most first-time owners dread, but it is a very simple business, particularly if your puppy gets used to it from an early age. A puppy's nails will need cutting or filing when they appear long and are starting to curve. The best method of holding the puppy for this task is to tuck the pup under your left arm, and hold one leg out with your left hand. Then, using the nail clippers in your right hand, just snip off the ends of the nails, being very careful not to go into the quick or they will bleed profusely. It is only the tip of the nail that needs to be removed. The easiest and safest method is to use a small metal car file, measuring about six inches in length. Then you can gently file the nails back, taking off as much as you want, without the risk of cutting the quick. You will probably find that your puppy accepts this method much more willingly.

EARS

Use a cotton bud to gently clean around the ear, just on the inside and not probing too deeply. Examine the inside of the ears, and if you can see any loose debris, try to remove it with the cotton bud, but again, do not go down too far into the ear. If the puppy is showing signs of having ear problems, such as scratching its ears or shaking its head, then take the puppy to the vet for a check-up.

Yorkies have about one-third of the hair on the back of the ear trimmed. This is quite a simple operation if you take care, and it certainly improves the appearance of you pet. This should be done by using a pair of scissors, and, holding the ear leather in your left hand, trim off the long hair around the top third of the ear. However, if you feel at all nervous about attempting this, take your Yorkie to a professional groomer.

FEET

Trim the long hair around the feet to neaten the appearance, and also trim the long hair underneath the feet around the pads. During the grooming and trimming, talk soothingly to your pet, with the aim of getting it to enjoy the attention. A contented well-trained dog will be so much easier for you later, rather than trying to fight with a wriggling unhappy Yorkie.

DISCIPLINE

The preceding tasks – lead training, grooming and bathing – are all forms of discipline and will all help to turn your puppy into a loving responsive adult. Further training can be undertaken at play times.

Call your puppy to you, and when it responds, give it a quick cuddle and plenty of praise. If it doesn't come when you call, don't worry; Yorkies are very independent and it sometimes takes a little while to learn this lesson. This is one of the most vital commands, so it is important that you persevere until the puppy obeys. Go and do something else for a few minutes, and then come back and try again. Eventually the puppy will respond, and you must reward it with plenty of praise. When the puppy does something naughty, like continuously yapping or chewing something it shouldn't (thank goodness, Yorkies are not great chewers), a sharp 'No' is normally enough to stop the puppy in its tracks. If this does not work, take the puppy away from the situation and distract it by giving it one of its favourite toys. This is far more successful than having a confrontation. Never smack your puppy; it is totally unnecessary.

THE GARDEN

Your garden should be completely enclosed: Yorkies are notoriously curious and they will always want to know what is on the other side of the fence, although I would not class them as a breed who will normally set out to escape and stray. However, it is best to be safe than sorry; you should check the fencing at regular intervals to make sure that no holes have appeared.

When your Yorkie is house-trained, let it out in the garden first thing in the morning, last thing at night, and at regular intervals during the day. People always ask whether the puppy should be put in the garden when it is very cold or wet. In theory, as long as it is not absolutely pouring with rain, a puppy will come to no harm if it is left outside for a few minutes. In practice, my Yorkies will go to the open door, sniff the air, and if it is raining or very cold they will quickly retreat, and they virtually have to be forced out to do just what they have to do.

TRAVELLING IN THE CAR

Yorkies should always be put in a travelling box in the car; this prevents them being thrown about with the motion of the car, and a roaming puppy could be a danger to the driver. The travelling box will also make an excellent bed for the puppy in the house; it stops all the draughts, and if you have visitors with small children, you can put your puppy in the box for a rest, out of harm's way. My dogs all love their travelling boxes and consider them their own little homes. As soon as your puppy has completed its course of inoculations you can start to take it out in the car. Short frequent journeys are best to begin with, gradually lengthening the duration of the trip until the puppy is confident and happy to travel.

HOLIDAYS

I know many people who will not go on holiday because they are worried about leaving their dogs with family or friends, or at a boarding kennel. This is very restrictive for the rest of the family, and it is not sensible, as at some time during the dog's lifetime an emergency could crop up when you will have to leave it, and I always think it is very cruel to suddenly leave an old dog at a kennel for the first time. It is far better to get the dog used to kennels when it is young, and, in my experience, most Yorkies adapt to them because they like the hustle and bustle, and they respond to the set routines, as all breeds do. However, make sure you visit the kennel well in advance of your holiday, so you check it over. It may be a good idea to look at several establishments, and ask some questions about how your pet will be cared for, such as:

1. Where will your Yorkie be staying?
2. Has the kennel got a covered run?
3. What type of diet is fed?
4. Can you take your dog's own bed and its own toys?
5. Will your Yorkie be separated from large dogs?
6. Is there a vet on call?
7. Are the kennels heated in the cold weather?

If you are not happy about any of the answers you get to these questions, or are not happy when you look around the kennels, then go and view some others. I can assure you that there are many very good kennels which cater very well for tiny dogs.

THE SICK YORKIE

If you suspect that your Yorkie is not well, make an appointment and take it to the vet. Listen very carefully to the vet's instructions and follow them to the letter. Just like humans, dogs feel the cold when they are not well, so its bed should be placed in a warm area or near a radiator. Make sure that it always has a bowl of fresh water available.

THE ELDERLY YORKIE

Yorkies often live to a good age – fifteen years is not uncommon – so as your friend and pet grows older, extra care is needed. Walks should be shorter, and an elderly dog should not be left in a wet condition after a walk. If it is very cold, the dog will appreciate wearing a little coat when it goes out. Its bed should be placed in a warm, draught-free place, and it should have a thick blanket in it. Meals should not be too heavy, or too big in quantity, as with less exercise your pet may put on weight, and this is an extra strain on its heart.

I get so much enjoyment from my elderly Yorkies, they seem so wise and clever, and they are such a delight. Of course, it always makes me sad to think that a dog is getting old and may not be as fast as it used to be, but there are so many memories in that dear little face. It has been a part of your life for so long, sharing the joys and the tragedies, always showing such love and trust – would that a dog could live forever! I believe the only way you can, in a small way, repay your beloved pet for all the joy that it has given is to make its twilight years happy and contented, and always have special consideration for your elderly pet. The day may come when you will have to make what will be one of your most difficult decisions. Perhaps the vet has suggested that it would be kinder to have your Yorkie put to sleep, because nothing more can be done to relieve its pain and suffering. Be brave, and remember that this is something that we are allowed to do for our pets when they are suffering, which we cannot do for humans. Do not let the little one suffer. People think that because breeders have a number of dogs, the decision is easier. Believe me, it is not – it is always a terrible heartbreak. The only thing that gets easier is that, with the knowledge coupled with the experience, we know that it is the right thing to do.

BUYING ANOTHER PUPPY

I am touching on this subject because I have been asked about it so many times after the death of a dog. There are several thoughts that seem to go through people's minds. Most common is the desire to replace the lost Yorkie with a replica. This, of course, can never happen. Each dog is totally unique, just like humans, and when people voice this thought, I try to gently explain that no-one can ever replace the dog that died, and perhaps more time needs to pass before they will be ready for a totally different bundle of fun and love. Other people ask if I think they should have another Yorkie immediately after their dog has died. I think in lots of cases this is a good idea, and, somehow, it is a compliment to their first dog. Others ask if it would be better to try another breed, so that the new puppy will not remind them of their first dog. I always respond by asking why did they buy a Yorkie in the first place? Naturally, they tell me all the things that we all love about Yorkies, and so they answer the question themselves! Ultimately, I refer everyone back to the beginning of this chapter on whether to buy a Yorkie, and so we come full circle. Whatever the decision is, I know that a Yorkie will always enrich its owner's life, as mine have always done – and will always do so, for as long as I own a dog.

Chapter Eight

THE BROOD BITCH
AND STUD DOG

THE BROOD BITCH

BUYING A BROOD BITCH

Before contemplating buying a brood bitch, a lot of thinking and studying should be given to the matter in advance. Do you really want to start breeding your own stock, with all the responsibilities that go with it? Breeding is a very time-consuming business: are you going to be able to be at home when the puppies are born, and do you have the time to rear a litter? Have you considered the cost of buying the brood bitch, rearing her, the stud fee, a possible caesarian operation, and last but not least, the actual rearing of the puppies, with all the expense that entails?

If you have decided that you really want to start breeding Yorkies, enquire at some of the top kennels, whether they have any puppies for sale that are potential brood bitches. Always be honest with the breeder and you are likely get a lot more help, which you will undoubtedly need in the future. Buy the best quality bitch for breeding that you can afford – the one that conforms most closely to the Breed Standard. This need not necessarily be the most expensive, although most reputable breeders know the worth of their puppies. Ask the breeder as many questions as you can think of regarding the background and pedigree of your bitch. Most breeders are only too happy to show you photographs of your puppy's ancestors, and to explain why they mated certain bitches to certain dogs, and what the result was. Apart from being extremely interesting, this sort of information will be invaluable to you in the future. There is an enormous amount to learn about every line, so any information the breeder can give you will be helpful.

The brood bitch should have a good spring of rib to allow room for the puppies, and she should not be narrow on the back end, or problems in whelping may ensue. Preferably, buy a bitch that is slightly larger than the show type, without being coarse. Remember that coat colour and texture are very important in the Yorkie, so again, buy a bitch that conforms as closely as possible to the Breed Standard. Occasionally, breeders offer good quality brood bitches for sale on breeding terms. The terms differ from breeder to breeder, and also from bitch to bitch, depending on the quality. However, in most cases the breeder will ask for a certain amount of

Ch. Ozmilion Hearts Desire (UK). (Ch. Ozmilion Premonition – Ch. Justaromance). A top brood bitch, dam to five British Champions. Bred and owned by Osman Sameja.
Thomas Fall.

Ch. Chandas Shonahs Girl (UK). (Ch. Ozmilion Distinction – Ch. Chevawn Sweet Shonah). Bred and owned by Mrs E. Leyton and Mrs S. Chiswell. Thomas Fall.

Ch. Beebee Mi Blaze (UK). (Ch. Blairsville Royal Seal – Heidi of Peppinoville of Bee Bee Mi). Bred by Mrs J. Mitchell. Owned by Joe Magri.

Thomas Fall.

money at the time, and then either one or more puppies back from one or more litters. The exact terms should be stipulated in the form of a contract; this avoids any misunderstanding later. The bitch will not become your property until the terms of the contract are complete; so you will not be able to transfer her into your name with the Kennel Club, until the breeder has received all the puppies that are stipulated.

There are several reasons why a breeder may offer a bitch on breeding terms. It could be that the breeder would like to keep the bitch for breeding, but does not have sufficient room to house her. Breeding terms would mean that the breeder can still benefit from the bitch's bloodlines without having the responsibility of caring for her. Or it may be that the bitch that is being offered is of extremely good quality and this is reflected in the price. If this proves prohibitive to the prospective buyer, the breeder may decide to part with the bitch on breeding terms, especially if the breeder considers that you will be offering the bitch a good home and that you are really interested in breeding. Personally, I do not like either buying or selling puppies on breeding terms; I feel that there can always be problems with the terms of the contract at a later date. However, I do not dismiss this arrangement out of hand, particularly if it is the only way the breeder will allow you to buy the bitch of your choice. In this situation both the breeder and the new owner should make sure that all the details are written into a contract that you both sign. For example:

1. The amount of the initial deposit.
2. The total number of puppies required by the breeder.
3. Stipulate which litter, or litters, these puppies are to come from.

4. What age should these puppies be when they are handed over to the breeder?
5. Who chooses the stud dog?
6. Who pays for the stud fee?
7. Who will have the choice of the puppies, and in what order?
8. When will you receive the registration and all the papers for the bitch?

GENERAL CARE AND REARING.

Before you buy your bitch, you should decide where you intend to keep her. Obviously, you will want her to become part of the family and to lead as full a life as possible, but it should be remembered that when she has her puppies, you will have to keep her in a whelping box. I think it is cruel to suddenly confine a dog that is not used to this treatment. The best solution is to keep a travelling box in a corner of the kitchen, and for some periods in the day, put her in the box for a rest. After a while the bitch will consider this box is her own little home, and when the door is left open, she will go in of her own volition. Later on, when you have to transfer her to a whelping box, it will not be such a shock.

Your bitch will not require any special treatment while she is growing and developing, just a normal, balanced diet, and, of course, plenty of exercise. Give her lots of love and attention, but do not spoil her too much, as the bitches that have the most trouble when whelping are very often those that have been totally ruined by their owners. Ideally, you want a nice, even-tempered bitch, that is used to responding to your commands. The bitch should be wormed regularly, every six months, to keep her free of internal parasites. This is most important for all dogs, but particularly for the brood bitch. Make sure that you keep all her inoculations up to date. While your bitch is growing and developing, you will have the time to study pedigrees and learn as much as you can about the different lines and the breed in general. Start to think about which stud dog you would like to use on your bitch when the time comes. So many people leave this until the last minute, and then it is all too easy to make the wrong decision. Talk to as many breeders as possible, and listen carefully to their advice.

CHOOSING THE STUD DOG

Selecting a stud dog is one of the major decisions that we as breeders have to make. There are numerous factors to take into account, and I hope that the following information will help you with your decision.

LINE-BREEDING: This is when a bitch is mated to a dog from the same line, with some of the ancestors common to both pedigrees. This is the method of breeding used by most successful breeders, although it is important to remember that not only are you doubling up on the virtues, you are also doubling up on the faults, so make sure that the line you are using is as sound as possible.

IN-BREEDING: This is when a bitch is mated to a dog from her immediate family, such as mother to son, or brother to sister. In-breeding should never be contemplated by the novice. A considerable amount of knowledge is required about every dog on the pedigree, for several generations back, so that both genetic faults and genetic virtues can be taken into consideration.

OUT-CROSSING: This involves mating a dog and bitch from two totally different lines. It is not really advisable as the results can be very mixed. The offspring tend to be larger, and of very different types. If a bitch has been very line-bred, then an experienced breeder may resort to this method to restore strength to the line. However, I have to say that they are more likely to mate the bitch within their line, but with fewer ancestors common to both lines.

The first time that you mate your bitch, it is best to take her to an experienced stud dog. Young dogs, with little or no experience, tend to be impatient, and this could frighten your bitch.

WHEN TO MATE THE BITCH

The correct age for mating a bitch tends to vary. Never mate a bitch who is not mature, who still looks and behaves like a puppy. Just as with humans, different dogs mature at different ages, and it can be disastrous to mate a bitch who is not ready – physically or mentally – to take on the responsibilities of motherhood. The puppies may not be properly formed, or the bitch may refuse to take care of her babies. It is not worth the risk for the sake of waiting for the next season.

Bitches usually come into season between six and nine months of age, but it is not unusual for them to be later. It is inadvisable to mate a bitch in her first season; Yorkies do a lot of maturing between the first and second season, and there is no point in rushing things. A bitch is usually ready for mating between fourteen and eighteen months of age, providing she has already had one season. If you are planning to mate your bitch, she must be wormed before coming into season. It is usually fairly easy to detect when a bitch is about to come into season. She will keep licking herself at the back end, and will become much more affectionate. The vulva becomes enlarged and hard, and a couple of days later she will start to bleed. Although the normal time for mating a bitch is ten to fourteen days after she starts bleeding, this can only be a guide, as bitches vary a great deal. One of my own bitches always had to be mated on the third day, and she was completely out of season by the fifth day.

Once the bitch comes into season, you will be well advised to check her every morning to note any changes, not forgetting to note down the date that she started bleeding. Take some cotton-wool and just swab the vulva. For the first few days the blood will be dark-red, paling in colour and amount as the days go by, until it is a pale-straw colour. The vulva darkens in colour and becomes very soft; this is the time when the bitch is ready for mating and will accept the dog. At this time the bitch will turn her tail to one side when touched at the back. Very occasionally, a bitch will have 'silent heats': this means that she doesn't bleed at all when she is in season. This is very difficult for the novice breeder – or for any breeder. The bitch's vulva will still enlarge, and her general demeanour change. The breeder must keep a very close eye on her to note the changes in the vulva, and when she starts turning her tail. Another method of determining the day of mating is to take a vaginal smear. The vet will test the smear and inform you of the best time to mate the bitch. If you are in any doubt, then this is the best method to use.

When exercising a bitch in season, do take care, or you will have every dog in the vicinity on your doorstep. It is advisable to pick her up when leaving the house, and carry her a little way, and to do the same on your return. This will stop her leaving her scent like a trail leading to the house. If you are planning a litter, the time of year should also be taken into consideration. Most bitches come into season at six-monthly intervals, usually the spring and the autumn. I always prefer spring puppies, as I am able to put then out in the garden when they are a couple of months of age. Fresh air and sunshine, even for a just few minutes every day, really does seem to make a difference.

A question that I have often been asked is how often the bitch can be mated, and until what age. The answer entirely depends on how healthy the bitch is. Never be tempted to mate your bitch if she is not in really tip-top condition. Ideally, a bitch should only be mated once a year, thus giving her one season of rest. The Kennel Club stipulates that a bitch should not be mated over eight years of age, but that rule covers every dog and every breed registered with the Kennel Club. I do not like to mate a Yorkie bitch over the age of five years, and I prefer her to have no more than three litters.

THE MATING

As soon as your bitch comes into season, you must telephone the owner of the stud dog. This is very important, as it allows the stud dog owner to book the dog for you and make the necessary arrangements. So many times people ring at the last minute, which is not only extremely inconsiderate but could also mean that the stud dog of your choice is already booked. When you are talking to the stud-owner it is a good idea to confirm the stud fee and method of payment. The stud fee is normally required at the time of mating, unless otherwise arranged. I always ask the owner of the bitch to keep in touch every few days, especially if they are new to breeding. This means that we know how the season is progressing, and the likely day of mating. When it gets near to the time of mating, the final arrangements can be made as to day and time. Most breeders will suggest two matings, with a day in between, especially if you have a maiden bitch. In most cases the bitch will be given a free mating at the next season if she fails to produce any puppies, although this must be ascertained with the stud-owner when you are booking the dog.

When the scheduled day for mating arrives, do plan carefully, and give yourself plenty of time for the journey. Put the bitch in her travelling box in the car, and take a clean towel with you for use after the mating. It is a good idea to plan to stop for a while before arriving at the stud-owner's house, in order for the bitch to have a drink and relieve herself. Whatever you do, do not let her off the lead! When you get to your destination, take the bitch to the house in her travelling box. If you haven't got a box, then tuck her under your arm. Do not put her on the floor until you are invited to do so.

The stud-owner will handle the dog, and you may be asked to hold your bitch. Stay calm and quiet, and this will help your bitch to remain calm – she will probably be wondering what on earth is going on! The dogs may stay tied together for twenty minutes or so, or they may not tie at all. A tie is not required in order for the bitch to conceive, but is preferable. Immediately after the mating, pick up your bitch, and wrap her back end in the clean towel that you brought with you. Give her plenty of praise, and put her back in her travelling box to rest. If she is a maiden bitch she has probably found the whole procedure quite traumatic.

A bitch will usually accept a dog for about four or five days – although this does vary considerably – and this is even after she has been mated. In fact, the bitch can become really flirtatious, and she may have to be watched very carefully to ensure that she does not escape from the garden, and go in search of another partner. I owned a bitch who detested my dogs when she wasn't in season, bossing them about until they were frightened of her – she really was quite objectionable. Imagine their shock when she came in season and flung herself at them! She wanted them to play, flirting and cavorting all over them. They were totally amazed and shocked at this sudden and total change, and could scarcely believe their luck. However, this is where I had to intervene and confine the bitch to her box before she drove all the dogs mad. The dogs looked at me as though I was a real spoilsport!

INFERTILITY

There are numerous reasons why a bitch does not conceive, but probably the most common is incorrect timing. Novice breeders are often so anxious not to miss the time when the bitch is ovulating that they present her to the stud dog far too early. Consequently she fails to come into whelp and there are no puppies. A dear, elderly gentleman, bought a brood bitch from me, and when the time came, he brought her back to be mated. I had warned him to let me know exactly when she came into season, which he duly did. I explained exactly what he had got to look for, and I said that the bitch would probably not be ready to be mated for another ten days. The next morning, the phone rang, and it was this gentleman, stating that he was sure that the bitch was 'ready'. I assured him that it was very unlikely, but in the back of my mind I recalled my bitch who always had to be mated on the third day of her season. We chatted for a while, and as he seemed so convinced, I suggested that he brought the bitch for me to look at. Of course, the bitch was nowhere near ready, but at least the old gentleman felt happier because I had examined the bitch. However, he did not let the matter rest there. Every single day he telephoned me, convinced that the bitch was 'ready', and I ended up nearly as anxious as he was! In fact, the bitch was not ready to be mated until the twelfth day, but happily she conceived and produced three delightful puppies. The moral of the story is that if you are in any doubt as to whether the bitch is ready to be mated, do phone the owner of the stud dog, who will be more than happy to help you. Some people find it difficult to discuss 'delicate' matters with a breeder, but please let me assure you that we have heard it all, and it takes an awful lot to shock us; of necessity we are very down-to-earth!

A reason for infertility can be a hormone deficiency or imbalance, and this may be helped with hormone injections from the vet. I am convinced that a bitch can fail to conceive if she is very anxious or upset at the time of mating. Other breeders may disagree, but I believe that if the bitch is very upset, the vaginal secretions become very acidic, and kill the sperm. Whether you subscribe to this or not, it is always important to try to keep your bitch as calm as possible at this time, if only for her own sake. I have already mentioned that a very spoilt bitch may fail to conceive. This is the Yorkie that is always fussed over by the owner, carried everywhere, and never made to do as it is told. In fact, it is treated like a spoilt child, rather than a dog, and this depresses the natural instincts, whether it be a dog or bitch.

PHANTOM PREGNANCY

This is very distressing, both for the owner and the bitch. After mating, the bitch shows every sign of being in whelp. She goes off her food, appears to get much larger, and in the latter stages she even makes her bed ready for the puppies. I had one bitch who made her bed, scratching up all her bedding all through the night; she was clearly convinced that she was about to give birth. I stayed up all night with her, and at 4 am she looked up at me and wagged her tail. Her face had a totally different expression, and when she walked towards me I could see that she had gone down like a pricked balloon. Both of us were very disappointed. When this happens it may be necessary to get some sedatives for your bitch from the vet, if she becomes very distressed.

THE STUD DOG

If you have started breeding Yorkies seriously, you may be tempted to keep a stud dog. I would not advise anyone with only a couple of bitches to do this, as it does bring its own problems, but if you have a few bitches, then it may be a good idea. The stud dog should have an excellent temperament. It does not matter how closely he conforms to the Breed Standard: if his temperament is unsound he should not be used at stud. When breeding, it is always wise to remember that most if not all the puppies will be going to pet homes, so temperament must be a prime consideration. Overall physical soundness is also essential. If an unsound dog is used frequently at stud, it can affect the whole breed for many years to come. Even if he is only used on a bitch once, the risks to the progeny are great. The dog should be typical of the breed, and as close to the Breed Standard as possible. If you are line-breeding, remember that the stud dog will hopefully stamp his attributes on his progeny, but it can take generations to find out just how dominant a certain dog is, whether for his attributes or his faults.

REARING THE STUD DOG

Like the brood bitch, the stud dog must not be spoilt, and while he should lead as normal a life as possible, he must also be obedient and of an even temperament. One of the first lessons that he must learn is that, although there are bitches in season in the near vicinity, they are not necessarily for him, and that he must not continuously bark and howl. Barking all day can be very wearing, both on the family and on the dog, and the dog will lose weight and condition very quickly. It is important to keep the stud dog free of worms and internal parasites, so he should be wormed every six months. It is also a good idea to bath the dog with an insecticidal shampoo each time that he services a bitch that is not your own. This is a precaution to ensure that he is not infected by any unwelcome visitors that the bitch may have brought with her.

TRAINING THE STUD DOG

When using your dog at stud, always keep to the same place and the same routine for the mating. Do not feed the dog for several hours before the mating, or he is likely to be sick all over the bitch. Trim the hair around the penis, so that entry into the bitch is easier, and afterwards the penis will retract into its sheath without the hair getting caught.

It is preferable to start training a Yorkie stud dog at about eleven months of age. Allow him to mate one bitch, and then do not use him again until he is about fourteen months old. Start with a steady, mature bitch, who has already had puppies. Never mate a maiden dog (one who has not mated a bitch before) to a maiden bitch, as the bitch could snap at him, and this could put him off for life. If it is at all possible, it is better to use one of your own bitches; it will give the dog more confidence if he knows the bitch. When it comes to the mating, allow plenty of time, and have a helper on hand. Start off by putting both Yorkies on the floor to play, and soon the mature bitch will start to flirt with the dog. Not knowing what he is doing, or how to do it, the dog will

Ch. Finstal Johnathan (UK). (Garsims Captain Moonshine – Finstal Evita). Sire of Ch. Finstal Sugar Icing (USA). Bred and owned by Sybil Pritchard.

Thomas Fall.

Ch. Patajohn Magic (UK). (Ch. Crosspins Royal Brigadier – Patajohn Merry Go Round). Bred and Owned by Pat Allington.

try and mount the bitch. This is the time to enlist the assistance of your helper to hold the bitch's head, while you kneel on the floor at the side of the bitch. When the dog gets really excited, he may try to mount the bitch's head, neck or back, so gently push him round into the correct position. At first the dog will probably object to this, and he may dismount from the bitch. However, it is important to persevere, by gently touching him on his rear end until he accepts it. One day he may have to mate a really difficult bitch, and it will be far easier if he is used to being handled or helped to enter the bitch.

If the bitch is a lot bigger than the dog, it may be necessary to put a thick book just behind the bitch's back legs to give the dog a step up. A little Vaseline, smeared just inside the vulva, may also help the dog to enter more easily. When the dog has entered the bitch, put your hand under his back end to hold him in position, as, if it is a large bitch, his legs may be off the ground. The thrust of the dog will be much stronger now, until he has spent himself. He will suddenly relax, and the dog and bitch will be locked together in the 'tie'. The tie can last up to twenty minutes or so, during which time the dog and bitch must be held. If one of them tries to pull away, it could damage the dog very badly. Holding the dog and bitch together on the floor, is a back-breaking job for the owner, and when the dogs finally break loose, you will wonder if you will ever stand up straight or walk again! To avoid this, I always let the dogs play for a while on the floor beforehand, and then move them to a table for the actual mating. Under normal conditions, once the dog is spent and they are tied together, the dog will try to turn. I train my dogs not to do this, but to stay resting on the bitch's back. If it is a large bitch and you allow the dog to turn, it would leave him hanging upside down, which would not be very comfortable for him.

Once the mating is over and the dog is released, give him lots of praise, put him back into his kennel, making sure that his penis has retracted into the sheath. After a little while give him a meat meal. If the bitch is not your own, make sure that you have written out the pedigree ready to give to the bitch's owner when they pay the stud fee. Officially, you have now completed your duties as far as the bitch is concerned, but I always consider that it is my responsibility to help the bitch's owner all through the pregnancy, whelping, and rearing of the puppies, in any way that I can.

Chapter Nine

PREGNANCY AND WHELPING

THE PREGNANCY

The average gestation period is sixty-three days from the mating, but this does vary, and many Yorkies whelp on the sixtieth day, and occasionally even earlier, so it is wise to be prepared. After the mating the bitch should return to a normal life for several weeks. Give her a well-balanced diet, but do not increase the quantity until two weeks before the puppies are due, at which time she will probably appreciate several small meals, rather than one large one. Exercise is important, but again, in moderation, and certainly no more than she would normally have. Between the third and sixth week after mating, most bitches go off their food. This can be a worrying time, but try not to get too anxious, as this will pass straight to the bitch, and she will become anxious too. Try to tempt her with a little chicken, or something that you know that she is fond of. All of a sudden, she will start to eat, and quickly make up for lost time. In fact, you will probably have the opposite problem.

At about five weeks into whelp, the bitch will have thickened around her middle and she will be starting to lose her waistline. When she is turned on to her back the abdomen will appear enlarged, with the nipples slightly swollen and pink. From this time onwards it is prudent to keep strict notes on all the changes that occur, however unimportant that they may seem to you at the time. If she develops any problems at a later stage, it will give the vet an overall picture as to how she has been throughout her pregnancy. These notes will also be invaluable to you for future whelpings; even now I still record everything about each bitch, and from time to time I find it helpful to refer back to them. The most certain sign of pregnancy comes at around six to seven weeks, when the bitch will develop a sticky, odourless discharge from the vulva. As the pregnancy progresses, the discharge will become slightly heavier. It is not until the last ten days of the pregnancy that the movement of the puppies can be felt. This can be done by turning the bitch on to her back, and then gently place the palm of your hand on her abdomen – you will feel a slight rippling of the abdomen.

This is the time to decide where is the best place for your bitch to whelp, before she decides for herself. There are many different types of whelping box, all with their own merits and disadvantages, from a large cardboard box to a very swish, very expensive, purpose-built whelping box. Obviously it will depend on your circumstances which one you opt for. The large cardboard box, providing it is sturdy, is perfectly suitable. You can just throw it out when it is dirty, and get a new one. I prefer a cardboard box to a wooden box. However careful you are with cleaning and disinfecting, germs will get into the wood, and this type is also very bulky to store. The manufactured UPVC whelping boxes are ideal. They are easy to clean and disinfect, they can be stored flat, and last but not least, they are designed to give easy access to the bitch while she is actually whelping, and afterwards when she is nursing the litter. However, they are expensive, and if you only have one brood bitch, you may not want to invest in one. For those who are going into breeding on a larger scale, this type of whelping box is invaluable – I would not like to be without mine. The whelping box should be situated in a place where it is fairly warm, and very quiet. I always have the whelping box in our bedroom, so that I can hear every sound during the night, just in case the bitch starts to whelp unexpectedly. It is also very quiet in there during the day, with the added advantage that the whelping and nursing does not disrupt the whole household. I start to get the bitch used to the new box and situation when she is about four weeks into whelp, and by the time she is seven weeks in whelp she should be used to spending short periods of each day in the whelping box.

At seven weeks – that is two weeks before the puppies are due – it is time to give the bitch extra calcium. This can either be given in tablet form or in liquid form, whichever you find easier, but it must be given regularly every day, and increased after the bitch has whelped. I always put a little cheese on top of the food at this time, and increase the meat content of the meal. Preparations for the whelping should be made well in advance; every whelping is different, and while there are guidelines to go by, one must always be ready for the unexpected. All the equipment that is required for whelping should be assembled.

WHELPING REQUIREMENTS

1. Plenty of newspapers.
2. A hot-water bottle.
3. Several old towels.
4. Antiseptic (a mild type such as Savlon).
5. A small cardboard box (large enough to take the hot-water bottle).
6. A reel of cotton thread.
7. Small scissors.
8. Notebook and pen.
9. Cotton-wool.
10. Vaseline.
11. A large plastic bag for the soiled newspapers.

It is advisable to give the expectant mother a general trim, not later than two weeks before she is due to whelp. If the coat is very long, it will be much better to cut it to a manageable length, bearing in mind that during the birth it may become very soiled, and afterwards the puppies could get it caught around their necks and strangle. Make certain that the bitch's nails are short, and that she is in a generally clean condition, with no matts in the coat. Some breeders advocate bathing the bitch at this time, but unless she is really dirty, I prefer not to at this stage. The bitch will be large and ungainly, and she could slip in the bath and injure herself. It would also involve

*The whelping box.
(Manufactured by
Snowsilk).
Alan V. Walker.*

the bitch having to stand for a considerable length of time while she is being bathed, dried and groomed. However, the hair on the belly must be cut off, paying special attention to the hair around the nipples, and around the vulva. This can be done easily if you turn the bitch on her back, while she is lying on your knee. Lastly make a solution of the antiseptic in a bowl, and with a pad of cotton-wool, gently wipe the whole of the abdomen and the vulva. Repeat this procedure every few days, until after the puppies are born.

THE EIGHTH WEEK

An average-size Yorkie bitch will generally produce between two to four puppies, although there are always exceptions to the rule – I know of one bitch who produced eleven puppies! However, if the bitch is carrying a large litter, she will now be getting very uncomfortable. She will not be able to stand for long periods, or to lie in one place for any length of time. Take her for only short walks, so as not to exhaust her, and give several small, easily-digested meals instead of one or two large ones. Every bitch reacts differently to this stage of pregnancy. Some bitches may be very heavily in whelp, but will still want to lead a perfectly normal life. This type has to be watched carefully to ensure that they do not leap off chairs, or any other high surfaces, or exhaust themselves by too much running about. Other bitches really take care of themselves and take the ante-natal period very seriously. They slow down considerably, and will not attempt to do anything that could be harmful. One of my bitches would start to waddle immediately after she had been mated, as though she was in heavy whelp. It was so comical to watch, but she was so easy to deal with. These types usually make by far the best mothers, and this particular bitch would foster orphan puppies, even when she did not have any puppies herself, coming into milk within twenty-four hours of being with them. At times, she was an absolute godsend, but unfortunately, she always considered that she could look after any puppies better than the actual mother. This was probably true, but if I didn't watch her very carefully, she would jump into any whelping box when the mother was out relieving herself. The first thing I would see was 'Madam', sitting as proud as punch with her new 'brood'! I must add that this type of bitch is definitely in the minority.

Any breeder will tell you that the most difficult in-whelp bitches are bitches that are, or have been, show dogs. They have had so much attention for so long, that they really believe they are above the mundane chore of producing puppies. They behave as though they were film stars, and you are at their every beck and call. They are used to the glamour of the show ring, with everyone admiring them, and to being waited on with slave-like devotion. The Yorkie is master of the art of looking down its nose at anything or anyone – and this is not quite so funny when you have got a show bitch looking down her nose with distaste after she has just produced (with much complaining) a beautiful litter of puppies!

Do not forget to keep giving the calcium supplement at this stage. It is of the utmost importance in preventing the bitch going into eclampsia, which is an imbalance of calcium in the body. This is a life-threatening condition, and some Yorkie bitches are prone to it.

THE WHELPING

FIRST STAGES OF LABOUR

The first indication that the birth process has begun is when the bitch becomes far more restless than usual. It will appear as though she cannot sit still for more than two minutes together. For the last week or so, she will have been scratching at the newspaper in her whelping box, but now the scratching will have more purpose to it, as though she has something definite in her mind; she may also begin to tear up the newspaper with her mouth. When she is sitting with you, she will look into your eyes imploringly, as though she is asking you to do something about her condition. This is a time when she will need you to be very calm – which will reassure her that everything is all right, and that she can rely on you.

I have seen novice breeders panic at this point, fearing what lies ahead. I find this attitude very self-indulgent, and I have little patience with the person who puts their own feelings above the feelings and well-being of the bitch. I recall one owner who was virtually hysterical when her precious bitch started to whelp. She phoned every breeder in the area, and called in the whole family, plus two vets. When she phoned me, there were so many people in the house that it sounded as though they were having a party. I advised her to get rid of all the people, except for one vet, and get the bitch calmed down. However, it was to no avail; this type of person worries more about their own feelings and always wants to have people around them. The outcome was that the bitch died, and, of course, the little orphan puppies were immediately shipped out to another breeder with a foster mother. Even as I write, I can feel the anger welling up in me again. The bitch may have died anyway, but she should have been given as much love and reassurance as possible, from her owner.

One other way of determining if the bitch has started to whelp is to take her temperature. Put a little Vaseline on to the end of a rectal thermometer, and insert it gently into the bitch's anus. The normal temperature for a dog is 101.5 degrees Fahrenheit, but in the last week of pregnancy it will fluctuate between 101.5 and 99F. If the temperature is 99F or less, then it should be taken again after half-an-hour. If the temperature remains low, repeat the procedure every few hours. If it remains at this point, then it is very likely the bitch will whelp within twenty-four hours. This method is not foolproof, and it should only be used as an indication, as the bitch's temperature may rise because an infection has started, or because she is in some way distressed. Unless you are very experienced, it is better to look for the outward signs.

In the twenty-four hours before whelping, the bitch will probably refuse all offers of food; the restlessness will be more noticeable, and she may start shivering. From this time onwards do not leave the bitch alone. It may be another twenty-four hours before she whelps, but as I have said before, every bitch is different, and things could start to move very quickly. Continue with your normal routine, just keeping an eye on how things are progressing. As soon as you see a mild contraction – that is when the abdomen hardens and then relaxes – take your bitch to her whelping box and make her comfortable. Note down any changes that you observe. As the contractions get stronger, the bitch will stretch out and brace her back feet on the sides of the whelping box. Between the pains she will become very restless and tear the newspaper up with her teeth, as though she wants to shred it. It is not unusual for a bitch to shake quite violently and pant. Some bitches go through it all by the book, while others have very few symptoms for you to go by. One of my bitches – Gaysteps Laura in Blue – whelped a litter, and the first indication that the birth was imminent was when she had an extremely strong contraction. Some three contractions later, she produced a puppy; she did not tear up the newspaper, and she had eaten her previous meal with relish. This type of birth does not happen very often, but it is as well to bear in mind that it can.

At first, the strong contractions will come a few minutes apart, but as the birth progresses they will come closer together, getting stronger and stronger all the time, until it appears as though all the bitch's strength is going into the contractions. The vulva will now be soft and flabby to the touch, and a sac of nearly colourless fluid will appear. If you touch the area just above the vulva, it will be soft, indicating the outer sac containing the fluid that has protected the puppies. This sac of fluid acts as an excellent lubricant for the birth canal, and facilitates the movement of the puppies along it, until they are expelled. Do not worry if this sac recedes into the vulva after a contraction; after a while it will become larger, and eventually it will split and expel the fluid. The bitch will turn and lick at the sac, and while it is preferable not to interfere too much, the longer that the sac remains intact the better. If it splits too early, the birth canal will dry, making it harder for the puppies to pass along, and it will be more painful for the bitch. This stage of the birth can be very exhausting for the expectant mother; the contractions will be almost continuous and very strong. If there is no sign of a puppy appearing within an hour or so, or if the bitch looks as though she is tiring, then professional help must be sought. Equally, the vet must be called if the contractions stop at any stage, and the bitch goes into inertia.

Usually the puppy will appear head-first, covered in another sac, although with Yorkies it is not unusual for them to come feet-first. With each contraction more of the puppy will appear, receding just a little between the contractions. Once this sac is split, it is imperative that the puppy is born quickly, in order for it to be able to breathe. If the puppy is very large, you may need to help the bitch. This is not a difficult procedure, but it should be undertaken promptly if the puppy is not making progress out of the vulva. Try and put some Vaseline just round the inside of the vulva, and using your left hand, roll the vulva as far as you can up towards the anus, over the body of the puppy. Then get some cotton-wool in your right hand, and put it round the neck of the puppy. Do not attempt to pull the puppy until the bitch is having a contraction, and then pull it downwards and under towards the belly of the mother. If the puppy is coming feet-first, then grasp the feet with the cotton-wool in the same manner, pulling with the contractions until the puppy is released from the vulva. Quickly and carefully, clear the nose and mouth of any mucus with a piece of cotton-wool so as to allow the puppy to breathe.

The placenta (afterbirth) is attached to the puppy by the umbilical cord, will still be inside the bitch, and it usually comes away a few minutes after the birth of the puppy. It is better to let the bitch sever the cord herself; she will chew and pull at it in such a way that there will be very little blood lost. However, if she is a maiden bitch and doesn't appear to know what to do, then you will have to do it for her. Squeeze the cord between your thumb and forefinger about an inch from the abdomen of the puppy and, on the side nearest the placenta, shred the cord with the thumb-nail of your other hand. Never cut it with scissors, or the puppy may bleed profusely from the cord and could die. The other method is to tie a length of thread tightly around the cord, again about an inch from the puppy's abdomen, and cut the cord on the side nearest the placenta. If the placenta has torn away from the puppy during the birth and has been retained in the bitch, a close watch must be kept to make sure that it is expelled. The bitch will eat the afterbirth if she is allowed to. I do not permit my bitches to eat more than one, as they are a strong laxative.

Once the puppy has been cleaned and dried, with a towel, replace the soiled newspapers with clean ones. Then return it to the whelping box and allow the bitch a little peace to enjoy her firstborn, at the same time keeping a close eye on her for signs of the next puppy arriving. The time between births differs greatly from whelping to whelping, from a few minutes to several hours. The important thing to remember is not to let the bitch get too exhausted or distressed. I do not like a bitch to go longer than two hours without some sign of the next puppy. When the contractions for the next birth are getting strong, remove the first puppy from the whelping box and put it into the cardboard box, containing the hot-water bottle covered with a blanket. This is to prevent the bitch inadvertently stepping on the puppy while she is in the process of giving birth. Immediately the second puppy is born, replace the first puppy with its mother while you are drying the second puppy in the towel. Repeat this procedure until all the puppies have been born.

Make certain that you count each afterbirth, so that if one has been retained in the bitch, you can call the vet. who will give her an injection to expel it, plus antibiotics to avoid any infection. When the last puppy is born you will see a noticeable change in the bitch. The anxious look in her eyes will disappear and be replaced with a very soft, contented expression. She will curl herself round her little brood, licking and nudging them with pride. The puppies usually start to suckle about two hours after they are born; the very strong ones will start even sooner. Occasionally there may be a pup that needs a little encouragement. Pick it up with your right hand, and with the left hand squeeze a little milk from the nipple. Put the puppy's nose to the nipple, and it will start to suckle. If there is a very weak puppy in the litter, you may have to hold it to the nipple until it has gained enough strength to latch on for itself, with its tongue wrapped around the milk sac.

Your new mother will now be very tired. Give her a drink of warm milk, tell her what a good girl she is, and allow her to rest. Under no circumstances let other people come in to look at the litter. After an hour or so, check again that all the puppies are suckling, and make preparations to freshen up the bitch. You will need a bowl of warm water with a little antiseptic in it (and I do mean a little), cotton-wool, a towel and a brush. Put a towel on the floor next to the whelping box, so that she does not get distressed by leaving the puppies, and lift the bitch gently on to the towel. Dip the cotton-wool into the antiseptic solution, and squeeze out the excess moisture. Then wipe as much of the soiling as you can from the hind-end of the bitch, the vulva area and the coat, without getting her too wet, or she will catch a chill. Brush the coat very gently, just enough to avoid it matting, and replace her with her puppies. This operation should not take longer than five minutes, or you will have a very upset bitch on your hands.

Always keep the whelping box scrupulously clean, replacing the newspaper each time that it is soiled. The bitch will have a discharge for a couple of weeks after the birth, and so this will need to be done regularly. Freshen the mother with the antiseptic solution every day, paying particular attention to the abdomen and vulva areas, and drying her thoroughly afterwards. For the first few days, give the bitch very light meals, such as scrambled egg or a little chicken twice a day. Of course, water must be available at all times. The calcium supplement must be given every day, according to the manufacturer's directions, until a week after the puppies have been weaned.

COMPLICATIONS

UTERINE INERTIA

This is when the bitch does not have any contractions, or they stop before either one or all of the puppies have been born. There are several reasons for inertia. If the contractions are very weak, and the whelping is not making progress into strong contractions, it is usually due to a hormone imbalance and the vet must be called. This type of inertia usually means that the bitch will require a caesarian operation, although the vet will undoubtedly try giving an injection of pituitary extract in an attempt to strengthen the contractions. If the contractions have been strong for a prolonged period of time and the puppy has not arrived, the bitch will become exhausted and the contractions will become weaker. Never allow the bitch to strain for so long that this occurs; it may be that the puppy is too large for the bitch to produce, or it is in an awkward position. Whatever the reason, the vet should be called if the bitch has been straining for two hours without success, or before, if she is showing signs of tiring. The vet may be able to manipulate the puppy out of the vulva to allow the whelping to proceed normally.

SHOCK

Very occasionally, the shock of the whelping may result in a maiden bitch rejecting her puppies. When this happens a lot of patience is needed in order to give the new mother reassurance and help. Give her a warm drink of milk, put her on a hot-water bottle for a little while, and keep telling her what a good girl she is. Give her a little time to recover, but do not leave her alone with the puppies. After some time has elapsed, put the puppies up to the nipples to suckle, gently talking to the bitch all the time, and hopefully this will stimulate her maternal instincts. Soon you will find she is taking more interest in her new brood and is becoming proud of them instead of frightened of them.

ECLAMPSIA

This occurs most frequently between the tenth and fourteenth day after whelping. It is a calcium imbalance, and if it is not treated promptly the bitch will die. At the onset, the bitch will shiver and appear very unsteady on her feet, her head may wobble and she may vomit. These symptoms progress into rigidity of the limbs, convulsions, loss of consciousness and death. The vet must be called immediately the first symptoms are observed, as time is of the essence. With this condition, the vet will give a large dose of calcium by injection, and providing the injection is given in time, the result is miraculous. In a very short period of time the bitch will have fully recovered. It is unwise to allow the bitch back with the puppies, and they will have to be hand-reared. Eclampsia can occur anytime from a week before whelping to a week after weaning. Giving a calcium supplement during pregnancy and after whelping helps to prevent this condition, and it is obtainable in several different forms:
Liquid: Callo Cal D – obtainable from a vet.
Powder: Stress – to be sprinkled on the food. Available at pet shops.
Tablets: Calci-D – also available at pet shops.

METRITIS

This is an inflammation of the uterus, caused very often by a retained afterbirth or a retained puppy. Several days after whelping, the bitch will not want to eat. She will have a high temperature and a discharge from the vulva, and she will be in quite a lot of pain. Professional help will be needed and you must call your vet. This is why it is very important to keep strict notes during the whelping, and to count the afterbirths. If you suspect that an afterbirth has been retained, then call the vet, as this could prevent the bitch developing metritis.

MASTITIS

This is an inflammation of the milk glands, and it occurs most commonly when the bitch has a lot of milk, and only a small litter of puppies. The milk congests in the milk glands and they become hard and lumpy, which is very uncomfortable for the bitch. This condition can be prevented by rotating the puppies on to different nipples to make sure that each milk gland is suckled in turn. However, if mastitis occurs, dip a small towel into warm water and drape it over the milk glands. After a few minutes remove the towel, and try and express some of the milk by squeezing the nipple between your thumb and forefinger. Continue to do this with each milk gland until they feel soft and the bitch appears more comfortable. If you are not be able to expel the milk, then veterinary help must be sought.

Chapter Ten

REARING A LITTER

POST NATAL

After the puppies are born and are dry, it is very important to check that they are always kept warm. The bitch's temperature will rise for the first few days after the birth, but this may still not be enough to keep the puppies warm. A litter that is not warm enough will feel cold to the touch; they will cry a lot, and will sound thoroughly miserable. Puppies generate very little heat of their own for the first week or two, so can easily sink into hypothermia. There are numerous heating appliances available on the market, which can be bought at any good pet shop. The main types are heating pads and heat lamps. I prefer the heat lamps, which can be hung over the whelping box at any height, depending on how much heat is required at any given time. The one disadvantage of these lamps is that they can dry the skin of the puppies, causing the skin to flake, a little like dandruff. The heating pads come in two types: one is manufactured in material, which I don't like because I feel that they cannot be cleaned properly; and the other type is manufactured in a type of fibreglass. I prefer not to use the fibreglass pad, as, although it can be disinfected easily, the amount of heat coming from the pad can vary with the weight on top of it. If there was a malfunction and the pad overheated, the consequences would be disastrous. I know a breeder who used this type of heating for her Dobermann litter. She went out shopping, leaving the litter of six puppies comfortably warm on the heating pad. On her return a little while later, she was horrified to find that the puppies had all piled on top of each other – as puppies do – and the pad had over-heated. Three of the puppies underneath were dead, a truly terrible tragedy.

If your puppies cry a lot and do not appear to be settling, it is usually for one of two reasons: either they are cold, or they are hungry. If you have ascertained that they are not cold, then check that they are getting enough milk from the mother. Put a puppy to the mother's nipple, and make sure that it latches on. The puppy should draw the nipple right into its mouth, and you should be able to see the tongue of the puppy wrapped around the nipple. As the puppy sucks there will be very little noise; it should stretch out and pump the breast with its front paws. If there are a lot of sucking noises, and the puppy does not latch on properly – constantly letting go of the nipple – then it is getting very little, if any, milk. If this is the case then you must check the bitch to make sure that she actually has come into milk, bearing in mind that it takes three days after the birth for the bitch to come into full milk. Occasionally, with a large litter, the puppies may squeak a little for the first night, although they will not cry continuously. In this instance, you should check your bitch. Take the nipple between your thumb and forefinger and gently squeeze, and a little milk should appear at the end of the nipple. If no milk appears after several attempts, then help from your vet may be needed. The stomach of a well-fed puppy should appear rounded on the sides and flat on the front, when the puppy is turned on its back. In fact, it looks rather like a frog! The litter will be very content, and will sleep virtually all the time that they are not suckling.

The bitch must be put outside at regular intervals to relieve herself. For the first few days you may find that she is reluctant to leave her new babies, and so she will have to be picked up and put outside. The bitch's absence will give you the chance to check the babies without worrying the mother, and also to clean the bed. During the day, it is best to get into a routine of putting your bitch outside every two hours. The bitch will quickly realise that her puppies are safe while she relieves herself. Yorkies are usually superb mothers, caring and protective with their young, keeping them spotlessly clean.

When the puppies are four days old, it is time for them to have their tails docked, and their dewclaws cut. There is a currently lot of controversy about tail docking, and it may become illegal before too long. There are already a number of vets who are refusing to dock tails. I would prefer not to comment on this, but if your vet is anti-docking and you want your puppies' tails docked, then get in touch with a breeder, who may be able to give you the name of a vet who will be willing to perform the operation. If possible, ask the vet to come to your house to dock the tails, so you do not have to take such young puppies into a surgery, where they could be open to infection.

For the first few days after the birth of the puppies, the bitch should be offered light, nourishing meals, that are easily digested, such as boiled chicken with the skin removed, or scrambled egg that has been cooked without any butter or fat, gradually increasing the amounts, and reintroducing her normal diet. Do not forget to give her the calcium tablets – one in the morning and one at night – and this regime should be continued until one week after the puppies have been completely weaned.

FROM ELEVEN DAYS

Between eleven to fourteen days, the puppies eyes will open. The breeder should get a dampened cotton-wool ball and wipe the eyes from the inside corner to the outside, in order to remove any mucus deposited there. It is quite fascinating to watch the puppies at this time. They cannot focus yet, but will look around with their heads in the air, and will appear to be almost squinting in their efforts to see any movement. A little later the ears will open, and it is from this time that the puppies will seem to grow and develop in leaps and bounds. Remember to check the length of the puppies' nails, and trim them if necessary. If the nails are allowed to get too long and sharp, the puppies will make the bitch very sore when they pummel her as they suckle.

THREE WEEKS

At three weeks the puppies will be up on their feet and walking round the box. They will be starting to play with each other, although they are still very tottery on their legs, falling over each other in a very comical way. Puppies really are great time-wasters – I could watch them for hours. At three weeks of age it is time to introduce some solid food into the diet. I always start with baby cereal, mixed in a proprietary brand of puppy milk. Firstly, wash your hands to make sure that they are scrupulously clean, and then dip your finger in the cereal and let the puppy suck it off – a very messy procedure. Once the puppy has got used to the taste of the food, offer a saucer of cereal. Repeat this with each puppy in turn, until all the puppies are eating from the saucer. I must warn you to make sure that you do not feed them on a carpet, because they are going to make the most wonderful mess, walking through it, sitting in it, and generally getting it all over themselves and each other! After they have finished, clean each puppy, using a damp cloth, and then return them to their mother.

For a few days, just give the puppies the cereal once a day, preferably first thing in the morning. For the rest of the time, of course, the litter will stay with their mother. After a few days, when they are eating the cereal well, you can introduce some meat at lunchtime. Start with best-quality minced beef, used for humans, and either feed it raw, or just scald it – I prefer to feed it raw. Roll the meat into a ball about the size of a marble in your hand, and then, keeping hold of the meat, let the puppy suck it. Make sure that the pup does not take too much into its mouth at one time, or it will choke. Again, repeat this with all the puppies in turn. You will find that the puppies really love the meat, but do not be tempted to give them more than the marble-sized ball, or you will find that they will get upset stomachs.

At four weeks, introduce another cereal meal at about 4pm, and when the litter is four and a half weeks old, offer another meat meal at 8pm, gradually increasing the amounts, so that after every meal you can see that their tummies are full, without being bloated. By five and a half weeks your puppies should be completely weaned. It may take slightly longer with very tiny puppies. However, this is not a cause for concern; the tinies are often slower, and it is better not to rush anything when it comes to feeding.

HAND-REARING

For various reasons you may find yourself in the unhappy position of having to hand-rear your litter. This is extremely hard work, and should not be undertaken lightly; it requires a great deal of time and energy, to say nothing of patience. However, I can think of nothing more rewarding than rearing a litter of puppies to six weeks of age. I always advise people with a bitch due to whelp, to be prepared for this emergency before the bitch whelps. Puppies have a habit of being born in the middle of the night, or on a Sunday, when it is impossible to buy all the things that you will need for hand-rearing.

REQUIREMENTS FOR HAND-REARING
1. A feeding bottle with extra teats.
2. A tin of top-quality puppy milk, such as Welpi.
3. Cotton-wool.
4. Baby oil.
5. Towels.
6. Sterilising liquid, such as Milton for babies.
7. A bowl for soaking the bottle.

The milk must be made up exactly according to the manufacturer's instructions, and the bottle and teats must be sterilised after each feed. I find the best method for bottle-feeding is to sit in a chair with the towel on your lap, and lift a puppy on to your lap, and hold it gently there with your left hand. Take the bottle of milk in your right hand, and put the teat to the puppy's mouth. If the puppy does not start to suck straight away, you may have to dip the teat in a little milk, so that the puppy can taste it. Make sure that the hole in the teat is not too large, or the puppy will drink too quickly, and this will cause digestive problems. It should take about ten minutes for the puppy to take enough of the milk, with a short rest in the middle.

A new-born Yorkie puppy should only take about half a teaspoon of milk at each feed, but this is only a rough guide, depending on the size of the puppy. When the puppy is full, its stomach will be rounded at the sides. It is better to feed less, rather than too much, and the puppies will soon let you know if you are not feeding them enough, crying before the next feed is due, just like a human baby.

After the puppies have been fed, I always rub their backs, as with a human baby, as it seems to help their digestion. Then, take a cotton ball dipped in a little baby oil, and gently stroke the stomach in a downward motion. This stimulates the puppy to pass water and have a bowel motion. You should note the state of the motion, as it will show how your puppy is coping with the food. The motion should be dark-yellow and formed; it should not be runny. If the motion is curdled and slightly green in colour, then weaken the milk mixture slightly at the following feed, and this should result in a normal motion. Always be guided on the amount you feed by the appearance and behaviour of the puppy, plus the motions.

For the first two weeks, the puppies must be fed every two hours, day and night. This decreases to every three hours (day and night) from fourteen days to twenty-one days, and at three weeks old, the puppies can go through the night from midnight until 6am. At three weeks it is time to start introducing other food, and weaning should be carried out in the same way as for ordinary puppies. At four and a half weeks of age, the pups should be having four meals a day, two meat, and two cereal, with a milk drink at bedtime.

SIX WEEKS

When the puppies are six weeks old, they should be completely weaned from their mother. I am always guided by the mother about this. Many bitches want to leave their puppies for short periods from about four to four-and-a-half weeks. By this time the puppies are starting to pull the bitch about when they are playing, and naturally she gets tired. This is the time to give her a break for a while, perhaps when the puppies are being fed. Gradually lengthen the time that she is away from them, until at six weeks they are weaned. This process should be gradual, for the sake of the puppies, and the bitch. However, it is most important that the puppies are fully weaned by this age, as they are now big and demanding, and if they are still feeding from her, they will be draining her strength.

After the puppies are weaned, keep an eye on your bitch to make sure that her milk is drying up. If the mammary glands (milk sacs) appear enlarged and full, and they are hard to the touch, then put her back with the puppies for no longer than two minutes. This is just long enough for them to draw enough milk off to relieve the bitch. After a few days the milk will dry up, and the bitch will feel much more comfortable. Remember to continue the calcium tablets night and morning, for a week after the puppies are completely weaned.

WORMING

The puppies and the mother should be wormed when the puppies are six weeks old. There are many brands of worming tablets and creams on the market. I always use Shirley's Worming Cream, because it is gentle on the Yorkie's stomach, and is easy to administer. The worming cream comes in tubes; it is available at most pet shops, and it can be given without starving the puppy first. All you have to do is squeeze a little of the cream on your finger (the amount is stipulated on the maunfacturer's instructions), and either put it on the end of the puppy's nose, so that the pup will lick it off, or, gently open its mouth, and just draw your finger gently along the roof of the mouth. Then repeat the procedure with the bitch.

FROM SIX WEEKS

This is my favourite age for the puppies; they are so amusing – feeling their feet, curious about everything, and pushing their luck with the other puppies – but it is also the time when a lot of work is needed to ensure their physical and mental well-being. The puppies will need a safe and warm place to live, now that they are away from the whelping box. I always put the litter in a pen, in a corner of the kitchen. I cover the floor of the pen with newspaper, and I provide a bed that is large enough for all the puppies, at one end. The advantage of keeping the puppies in the kitchen is that they are able to watch everything that is going on, and they get used to all the noises of a busy household. It is their first step into the grown-up world.

DIET AT SIX WEEKS

8am. Cereal and milk.
12 noon. Minced meat, with a very small amount of biscuit mixed in.
4pm. Cereal and milk.
8pm. Meat and biscuits.
10pm. A drink of milk.
Water should be available at all times.

SIX WEEKS TO THREE MONTHS

When your six-week-old litter of puppies are happily settled in their new pen in the corner of the kitchen, with plenty of toys to play with, it is a wonderful time to watch them. Their different characters are beginning to develop, and their intelligence starts to show in the way that they play. However, this is the time that they need a lot of attention and time spent on them. Mealtimes are hilarious; they get so excited while you are preparing their food, and when you put it down for them there is a jostling for the best position, or what they consider the best position. Make quite sure that each puppy gets its fair share – the quieter ones sometimes get pushed out.

DIET AT THREE MONTHS

8am. Cereal and milk.

Konig puppies (Malaysia) aged eight weeks.

Nelmila Berryfield Rosebud (UK) aged fourteen months (Nelmila Joab – Nelmila Berryfield Ruth). Bred and owned by Ivy Millard.

1pm. Meat and biscuits.
6pm. Meat and biscuits.
9pm. A drink of milk.
Water should be available at all times.

You can check if you are feeding the correct amount by picking up each puppy individually, and making sure that its tummy is rounded at the sides, but flat on the front. If its stomach is not rounded at the sides, the puppy is not getting enough food. On the other hand, if the stomach is rounded at the front to the point of bulging, the puppy is eating too much. It is important not to over-feed, and to judge the amount that you feed at each meal by the appearance of your puppies. Never leave food down for the puppies from feed to feed. If they have not cleared their plates in a few minutes, then it means that you are feeding too much. If this happens, pick the food up and throw it away, and then feed them a little less at the next meal.

Once the puppies have left their mother at six weeks, you will need to start bathing them. (I have explained how to bath Yorkies in detail in Chapter Seven: The Companion Yorkie.) The puppies will need to be bathed every two weeks, although you will find that at six weeks of age, their coats will become sticky and unpleasant after feeding – no matter how much you try to clean them after each meal – and they will require a bath more often.

During this time the puppies will be teething, so make sure that they have plenty of safe toys to chew on. I find they get a lot of fun from playing with a pair of lady's tights, folded and tied in the middle, and these are ideal for games of 'tug of war'. The puppies must be watched very carefully, to make sure they do not harm themselves in any way. It is very beneficial if they can be allowed the freedom of the kitchen for a while, or anywhere else where you can supervise them, so long as you keep a very close eye on them. Make sure that they do not jump from chairs, or up and down the stairs, as they will land with their full weight on their front legs and could very easily break them.

After about eight weeks, if it is a lovely, warm day, the puppies can go into the garden in their pen for a little while. Make sure that there isn't anything on the ground that will harm them, and nothing that they could eat and choke on, or anything that is poisonous. Place the pen under a tree, or in some shade. Never leave the puppies in full sun, as they can get heatstroke, just like us.

All too soon the time will come when you have to decide which puppies you are going to keep (if any), and which ones you are going to sell. I consider the best time to sell a puppy is at ten weeks. At this age, the pups are well on their way to independence, and they have been away from their mother for four weeks. However, there are numerous things to do before the little ones can leave your home to start their new life. Firstly, check with your vet to see if any inoculations are due, or can be given to the puppies, such as the parvo virus inoculation, and also ask the vet to check the puppies over for you, to make sure that they are sound and healthy. The pedigrees will need to be written out for each puppy, and the registrations must be sent for from the Kennel Club. It is your decision whether to register the puppies or not – and it is a decision which should not be undertaken lightly. However, if you decide not to register them, prospective buyers must be told before they commit themselves to buying a puppy.

A diet sheet should be written out for each puppy, including details of your general routine, times of feeding, when to bath, when the puppy must have its next inoculation, and any little thing that you think will help the new owner to settle the puppy into its new home more easily. It also helps if you can give diet sheets for the puppy as it gets bigger.

DIET AT SIX MONTHS

8am. Meat and biscuits.
6pm. Meat and biscuits.
8pm. A drink of milk.
Water should be available at all times

DIET AT TWELVE MONTHS – ADULT

Many breeders only feed their Yorkies one meal a day after the age of twelve months; however, I feel that they have very small stomachs, and are better and happier with two small meals, morning and evening.

All the paperwork should be completed well before any prospective buyers come to look at the puppies, otherwise you will be in a fluster and a rush. When you are selling a puppy you need to be cool, calm, and collected.

THE PUPPIES LEAVE HOME

Well, your babies are now ten weeks old, and it is time for them to leave. It will be a sad time for you, as by now you will have become very attached to the little ones. These feelings are important when it comes to deciding whether the prospective owners are suitable to have one of your puppies. These people are coming to look at your puppies, but it also gives you the opportunity to assess them as possible owners. Sometimes, for no good reason, you may take an instant dislike to someone, and this is a situation that has confronted most breeders.

I remember a young couple phoning me and asking if they could look at some puppies. An appointment was made, and they duly arrived. They had all the criteria needed to own a puppy – a fenced-in garden, the wife didn't go to work, etc. – but I just didn't like the wife. I couldn't give any particular reason; I just didn't like her, and I didn't want any of my puppies going home with them. I was getting more and more worked up, as there was not a single reason why I should refuse to let them have a puppy. Then suddenly, the woman looked down at the puppies, screwed up her nose, and said that she didn't like Yorkie puppies. She said she thought they were ugly, and she only liked them when they were adult. That did it – I looked at her, and said that I didn't like her either, and I thought she was ugly! How dare she say that these little bundles of sheer delight, the apples of my eye, were ugly? Of course, they left in a great hurry, without a puppy. Afterwards I was somewhat ashamed of myself, and my husband was positively mortified. However, the moral of this story is to be prepared in case you don't like the people or you do not think that they will make suitable owners. Don't wait until you get really upset before you say anything, like I did. Instead, stay calm, and say that you are very sorry, but you have to consider what is best for your puppies, and you do feel that a Yorkie is not for them. Naturally, the people will be upset, but that is definitely better than insulting them!

When a puppy is sold, to all intents and purposes it no longer belongs to the breeder, but I always tell the new owners that if they have any problems with the puppy, either when they first take it home or later (and that means at any stage throughout its life), I will always be pleased to help, or just hear how it is doing. In my heart, every puppy that I breed will always be mine.

Chapter Eleven

GROOMING AND BATHING A SHOW DOG

There is no doubt grooming and presenting a Yorkie for the show ring is an art; it requires complete dedication, time and patience. The standard of presentation in the ring today is exceptionally high, and while we can all learn the method, and with practice we can improve, there is no doubt that there is an indefinable quality which makes some far better than others. I believe that the people who do reach the highest standards are the type who are self-motivated and meticulous about detail, with an eye for beautiful things, and total dedication to our glamorous breed. Do not let this put you off, dedication only comes with time, as does experience. If it is any consolation, most, if not all owners, ruin the coat of their first show dog while they are learning – myself included. Most top breeders will advise you: "Learn with your first dog, and then put into practice what you have learnt with your second." Even when you are

an expert at grooming, it does not mean that all will be easy. On the contrary, we all have owned show dogs who are determined not to have a long coat!

One of mine who immediately springs to mind, was a very beautiful bitch, and I had high hopes for her. The night before we were due to go to the Richmond Show, which was then held in London, I bathed her and crackered her up, all ready for the next day. The following morning we got up at the crack of dawn in order to make an early start. I let the bitch out of her box to relieve herself, and she came out just full of herself. I could not believe my eyes – she had chewed every single cracker off her coat – and she was standing in front of me with only an inch of hair left on her body! I sat down and sobbed, two years work down the drain, or to be exact, in the box. This experience was a great

Ch. Mistangays Boom Boom Mancini (USA) showing a tremendous wealth of coat. Owned by Barbara and Ron Scott.

*Ch. Phalbrienz Tamarix
(UK) groomed to perfection.
(Ch. Ozmilion Sensation –
Ch. Rozamie Endless Love).
John Hartley.*

leveller for me, as dogs always are, and I had to console myself that at least she was happy, and that was the most important thing, after all. I can look back and laugh at this incident now, but at the time I could have willingly wrung her neck!

To raise a Yorkie from the nest, through its many stages of changing, to a beautiful full-coated dog, is rather like an extremely difficult obstacle course, but if you manage to complete the course, there is nothing to compare with the feelings of pride and exhilaration. This is what spurs us on to start again with another puppy.

REQUIREMENTS FOR DAILY GROOMING

1. Grooming table: This can be a small table, such as a card table, or a professional grooming table.
2. Stainless steel comb: This must be in perfect condition, without any chips, or it will damage the coat.
3. Pure bristle brush: This can either be obtained from antique markets or from stalls at the various club shows; it is the type of brush that used to come in a set for ladies to display on their dressing tables.
4. Rubber-bands: To hold the crackers in place.
5. Acid-free tissue paper: This must be acid-free so that it will not damage or change the colour of the coat. It is available at stationers.

6. Nail-clippers or file: Nail clippers are available at pet shops. The file, which is metal and about six inches in length, is the type used on cars, and can be obtained at car accessory shops.

7. Scissors: These must be sharp and the true hairdressing type.

8. Almond oil: To protect the hair, available from chemists or club stalls.

9. Small brush: To apply the almond oil to the coat; I always use a baby brush, available at any chemist.

10. Saucer: For the oil.

11. Cotton-wool.

12. Gauze finger bandage: To put over the paws of the Yorkie's hind feet, to stop it damaging the coat by scratching. This can be obtained at any chemist.

13. Microtape: To keep the gauze in place.

Training must begin at a very early age. I start to put my puppies on a table, virtually when they begin to walk about, not because they need much grooming at this age, but simply to get them accustomed to the feel of the table and being off the ground. This is also a good time to get the puppy used to lying on its back on your lap, and tickling its tummy. Hopefully, this will mean that as the pup gets older it will happily stay in this position when its underside is being groomed and its feet are being attended to. A couple of minutes 'training' a day is all that is needed, and you will find that your Yorkie will accept the situation. Of course, you will not know yet whether your puppy is going to be show quality, but this sort of training is good for any puppy, show dog or not. By the time I sell my puppies, I have them trained to be groomed on a table, without any fuss, so that it gives the new owners a head start. Never try to rush the training; the aim is to progress slowly but surely. Your ultimate goal is to have a dog who is content to stand and be groomed for long periods of time, and this is only achieved by a great deal of patience and feeling for your dog.

From six weeks of age, bath your puppy every ten days to two weeks. A clean coat is a growing coat, and everything must be done to help it. Diet is equally important. This should be well balanced, and should include some white meat and rice. Too much red meat overheats the blood and can cause the puppy to scratch, which is fatal for a show coat. A show dog must also be at the peak of fitness. Regular showing is very gruelling, so exercise is also crucial (see Chapter Twelve: Training and Exhibiting.) Get your puppy into a strict routine of being groomed every day. While it is on the table, brush the coat through very gently so as not to pull the hair, then carefully comb the coat. Clean the eyes with eye-drops such as Optrex, and check to see that the nails are not too long, clipping or filing as necessary. When the puppy is about three months old and is standing on the table for about ten minutes at a session, start applying a little almond oil to the coat. Pour about a half-a-teaspoonful of the oil into the saucer, and with the baby brush just dipped in the oil, brush it into and through the coat. Do not over-oil, as this will do more harm than good. Start with the head, and brush upwards from above the eyes, then downwards down the muzzle and the sides of the face, and then repeat on the back coat. The most common mistake in grooming is to use too much oil, thus clogging the hair, so do not re-apply the oil until you feel the coat starting to dry out, which usually takes several days. Unfortunately, because every coat texture is different, I cannot give the exact amount of oil to use, but generally the softer and finer the coat, the less oil you will need. Everything you do when grooming must be undertaken with the preservation of the coat in mind. A Yorkie's coat takes over two years to grow to maturity, and you really only get one chance to get it right.

At about five months of age, depending on how fast the coat is growing, it is time to begin the crackering. This is the term used for wrapping the hair in the acid-free tissue paper in order to protect it. This is one of the biggest hurdles in grooming, and never be tempted to commence it until you have the time to be with the puppy for most of the day. Remember to stay calm and keep your patience. It is vital that both you and the puppy are relaxed during this training period – you don't want to turn the puppy into a nervous wreck. Temperament is so important; many people expect too much from these youngsters, and seem to forget that, first and foremost, the puppies should be our much-loved pets.

Before starting the grooming session, fold each paper in half, lengthwise, and then fold an inch of the doubled paper over at the top. Groom the puppy in the usual manner, brushing and combing through the coat. Then, with the puppy facing you, part the hair on one side of the skull, taking a line from the corner of the eye to the middle of the base of the ear. Comb it up and hold it in the left hand, and then repeat the process with the opposite side of the head. You now should have all the hair on the skull in your left hand. Gently manoeuvre the head down a little, and part the hair between, and slightly towards the back of the ears, drawing the hair up into your left hand with the hair from the skull. With the right hand, place the paper (with the inch doubled over) at the base, behind the hair in the left hand, and fold it lengthwise around the hair, first around from the left and then around from the right. Run your fingers up the paper to make a crease up each side, then fold it over from the top several times, and wrap a rubber band around it to hold it in place. This sounds very complicated, and at first you will find it very awkward. However, it will be much easier if you follow the photographs and practise on a few strands of wool, until you are doing it with ease.

Once the cracker is in place, keep the puppy on the table for a few more minutes, and part the coat down the centre of the back and brush it down each side. Before putting the puppy back down on the floor, check to make sure that you have not pulled the hair up too tight in the cracker, which would feel very uncomfortable. Each dog is different: some take to the crackers as though they had been born with them, others take time to get used to them, a very small minority will never accept them, especially on the head and muzzle. These are the heart-breaking ones; you will just get a little coat and they will rip it out. Then you have to make a decision: do you want to carry on and make both your lives a misery; do you carry on and show it for a while in the hope that it will eventually accept the crackers; or do you stop showing the dog all together? I would advise anyone in this situation to keep on showing the dog until you have another one to replace it in the show ring. Try to stick to the small shows, where there will be less competition. On the practical side, I would suggest that you put slightly more oil in the coat, and stop crackering.

Most puppies attempt to take out the crackers at first. Watch your pup carefully, and say "no" whenever it attempts to scratch or rub on furniture or carpets. If the puppy succeeds in getting the cracker out, then replace it immediately. Do not get cross or make a big fuss, just replace it as though it is part of a day's work. For the first few days you will probably have to do this many times, but eventually the puppy will get used to the feel of it and forget it is there. It may be several weeks, or even months, before the rest of the coat will be long enough to go into crackers. In the meantime, continue training the puppy on the table. It is important not to cracker the hair until it is long enough to go into the papers easily. Do not be tempted to pull the hair tight to get it into the crackers – it will only break. If you remember these few rules of crackering, it is less likely that you will damage the coat:

1. Do not apply the oil down to the skin.
2. Too much oil will break the hair.
3. The coat must never be allowed to get too dirty and clog.
4. Always cracker to the shape of the dog, so that it is able to move without pulling the coat or feeling uncomfortable.
5. Do not cracker too tightly.
6. Bath regularly, every ten days to two weeks.
7. If one of the papers has come loose and is just hanging, replace it immediately.
8. Do not allow the dog to rub or scratch.

OILING AND CRACKERING (WRAPPING) THE COAT
Demonstrated by Anne Fisher and Gaysteps Golden Haze at Shianda, owned by Shirley Davies and bred by Anne. Photos: Bob Fisher.

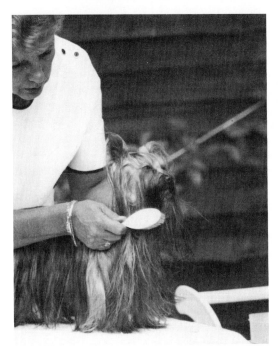

Using a soft baby brush, apply the oil to the coat and then comb through.

Always begin with the topknot and face. Comb and draw the hair up into the left hand. Place the paper behind the hair, then fold it round the hair first from the left, then from the right. Hold it in place at the base with the left hand.

Using the right hand, fold the cracker downwards, and continue to fold downwards until there is a neat 'parcel' on top of the head.

Secure the cracker with a rubber band – this should not be twisted too tightly.

Move to the side of the mouth and under the chin for the next crackers. Place the hair in the centre of the paper and fold the paper round the hair, first from the left, then from the right.

Fold the paper and secure with a rubber band. Ensure that only the hair from the upper lip – not the flesh – is caught into the cracker. (Always double-check these points).

Using the same method of parting the hair and then inserting the paper and rubber band, move round the dog until all the hair is wrapped in papers.

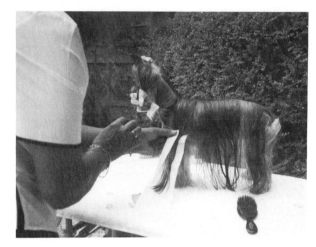

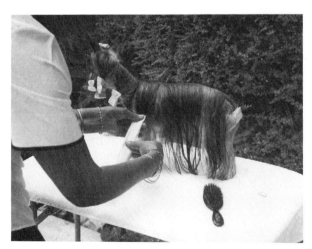

Normally four crackers on each side of the body are sufficient. Remember to always hold the paper containing the hair securely in position with the left hand, while working with the right hand.

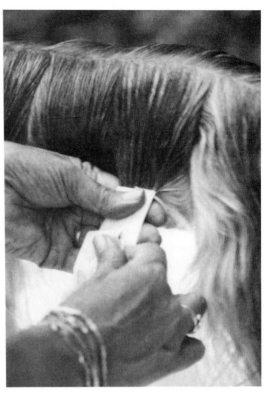

Make sure that the partings are situated to allow freedom of movement, i.e. just in front of a joint or just behind a joint; never over a joint as this will cause hair breakage and be very uncomfortable for the dog.

Check at all times that the hair is not being pulled too tightly into the paper.

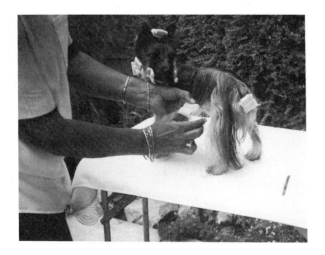

Adjust the size of the paper to the amount of hair to be wrapped, i..e. put a slightly smaller cracker into the tail coat and the hair on the legs.

When the crackering is completed, put either finger-gauze or little cotton boots over the back feet and secure them – not too tightly – with micropore tape or similar. The boots are put on the feet to prevent hair breakage should the dog scratch and catch its nails in the coat. Occasionally a Yorkie will pull at the head crackers with its front feet. In this case, boots will be required for all four feet.

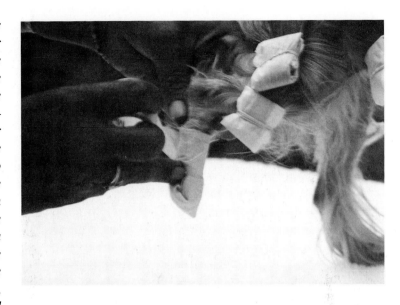

If you groom quietly and methodically, the Yorkie should become completely relaxed.

All the crackers are now in place.

Gradually, over a period of several weeks, you can cracker more of the coat, ensuring that, each time you add more papers, the dog has accepted them before you add any more. Bearing in mind that it only takes one good scratch to ruin a coat when it is crackered, it is wise to put 'boots' on the hind feet in order to avoid this. Put two layers of the finger bandage over the feet, going up to just under the hock, and secure it with microtape.

Now that you have your dog in full crackers, the grooming regime is very strict. The papers must be taken out each day, the coat combed through, adding more oil if necessary, and then the papers must be replaced. Inspect the boots to see if they are worn through or very dirty, and if this is the case, they will have to be renewed. Always keep the ear leathers clean, both inside and outside, and free from any oil, or the dog will develop stripped ear (see Chapter Fourteen: General Health Care). This is a very irritating condition, and it is far easier to prevent than to cure. Keep all your grooming equipment in one place, near at hand, so that any papers that need to be replaced can be attended to with a minimum of fuss. Our show dogs need so much time and attention that we must make the task easier wherever we can.

BATHING REQUIREMENTS

1. Bicarbonate of soda: This should be mixed to a paste with a little water in a saucer, and it is used for cleaning the teeth.
2. Baby shampoo.
3. A good-quality shampoo, either for dogs or humans. Never use an anti-dandruff shampoo – it

is too strong.
4. Hair conditioner.
5. Two towels.
6. Free-standing hair-dryer.
7. Grooming box with all the brushes, combs and tools, meticulously washed, and new papers ready-folded.
8. Cotton-buds, for cleaning the ears.
9. Cotton-wool.
10. Eye drops (Optrex).

Never use a brush or a comb that has oil in it on a clean coat. I have two sets of equipment in two different grooming boxes: one is the set that I use every day with the oil, and the other set is kept for shows and after bathing, and this is washed every time that it is used. The first step is to place your dog on the table and take out all the crackers and remove the gauze boots. Then, using the brush and comb from your daily grooming box, carefully comb the hair through without pulling it. Take a pair of scissors, and trim the hair off the ears, a third down from the tip – inside and outside – and then neaten round the ear where you have trimmed. Next, take a cotton-bud and clean just inside the ears, clip or file the nails, and trim the hair around and under the feet. Do not attempt to cut any other hair on any part of the dog until after it has been washed – the oiled hair changes shape dramatically when it has been bathed. Clean the eyes with Optrex and cotton-wool. The teeth should be cleaned by dipping a little cotton-wool into the bicarbonate of soda paste and gently rubbing the teeth with it. There are toothpastes on the market specially manufactured for dogs, but I find this method superior for removing any plaque that has formed. Finally, place a ball of cotton-wool into each ear to prevent water or soap entering the ear canal.

First wet the hair thoroughly on the head and face, taking care to avoid the eyes and nose. Apply some of the baby shampoo, squeezing it through the hair, and paying special attention to the muzzle and chin coat. Leave the shampoo on the head and wet the rest of the dog with water, working from behind the ears to the tail. Be careful not to rub the coat, as this will cause it to tangle. Use the palm of your hands and go down each side of the body from the centre parting, squeezing the coat gently as you go. This method takes a lot longer but is worth the effort. Next, apply the normal shampoo in the same manner, not forgetting the underside, legs and genital area. Carry on squeezing the coat and running the palms of your hands down it, until you have removed as much of the oil as you can. Rinse and repeat this procedure. If the hair is very clogged with oil you may have to shampoo a third time in order to remove all traces of it. When you have ascertained that there is not a hint of oil remaining, rinse thoroughly until all traces of the soap have disappeared. Apply the conditioner in exactly the same manner as the shampoo, again working from the nose to the tail. The amount of conditioner that is needed will entirely depend on the health and texture of the coat, and this is only learnt by trial and error. Never try anything new on the coat the night before a show – leave your experiments for the intervals between shows! Leave the conditioner in the coat for a few seconds and then rinse thoroughly several times. Finish by gently squeezing all the excess water from the dog, remove the cotton balls from its ears, and wrap it in a towel.

Again, I must emphasise that you *never* rub the coat with the towel under any circumstances, or you will end up with a tangled mess and some broken hair. Use the clean brush and comb, and put the hair-dryer on medium-heat and brush the coat as it is drying, which helps to prevent it waving. Once the coat is completely dry, comb it through to ensure that it is tangle-free and put the topknot up in a rubber-band. Comb through the hair again, while holding the dog's head in the correct position, to determine whether the coat needs trimming. During the summer, when the shows are held outdoors, the coat needs to be kept just to floor-level in order that the dog will not trip over it while it is moving across the grass. If there is too much coat on the ground, it also tends to drag the dog back and hinder the movement. In winter, when you are attending indoor venues, leave the coat to grow to about an inch on the floor. When you are trimming the coat length you will need to enlist the help of another person to make certain that the dog remains in the correct position without moving, while you are cutting. Comb the hair evenly down all round the body, then cut the hair to the required length. If you are exhibiting the following day, cracker the coat back up in clean papers. If not, re-oil it and cracker as usual, not forgetting to replace clean gauze boots. When the bathing is completed, allow your dog out to relieve himself, watching to make sure that it does not get dirty. Before retiring to bed, pack your show box and all your other requirements for the following day, so that you will not have a last-minute rush.

Chapter Twelve

TRAINING AND EXHIBITING

TRAINING

There is a saying in the dog game that prizes are won at home and not in the show ring. While this is not literally true, it is certainly a fact that if you don't put the necessary work in at home, your dog will not win in the ring. All aspects of training must be undertaken with meticulous care in order to produce a successful show dog. Try to imagine how the dog feels and thinks; you cannot explain things to it – it will not understand; so the dog must therefore have the utmost trust and confidence in you. Never allow yourself to let the dog down, never put it into a situation that it cannot handle; you must both learn to work as a team where you each know what the other is thinking. When this pinnacle of training is reached there is nothing more enjoyable for you both, but it is only achieved with time and patience. There are many aspects to consider when preparing a dog for the show ring. It is not enough to have an animal that does everything that is required of it by its owner when it is on the move, and stands like a statue when being examined by the judge. The dog must appear to be glowing with health, animated, with a zest for life that cannot be ignored. None of this just happens; it must be worked at from the beginning, taking each part independently, and culminating in a dog that is as near to perfection, both mentally and physically, as you can produce.

TEMPERAMENT

Temperament should be worked on from the nest. It is essential with any puppy – show dog or not – that they are happy, lively and full of confidence. This begins when you start to pick the puppies up and handle them – they are getting used to a human being as opposed to their mother. When they are few weeks old, give each puppy a few minutes on the grooming table, and gently brush its coat. A puppy should be introduced to all new situations gradually, and as it gets older and has had its inoculations, it should be allowed to meet as many people as possible. The local ringcraft classes are excellent not only for training, but also for socialising the puppy with other dogs and people. If, during any part of the training, you find that the puppy is nervous of something, do not be tempted to avoid that situation re-occurring. Take the time to gradually

Like all experienced exhibitors, Ronny Engelen (Belgium) starts training his puppies for show at a very early age.

Training pays off – this youngster became Ch. My Precious Love Trouble.

accustom the puppy to whatever it is frightened of. This method has a two-fold benefit: firstly, the puppy will learn to overcome its fear, and secondly, it will confirm the puppy's confidence in you – a goal that you must always be working towards when you are training. Once the puppy has total confidence in you, it will be so much easier to train, and it is far less likely to develop phobias. Never forget that although you are training a potential show dog, you also have a perfectly normal, little puppy, who will want to play and explore and get into mischief. Playtime is as essential for its mental and physical well-being as training, and very often the two can and must be combined.

A show box or travelling box is very useful, and should be used to its full advantage. Never allow your dog to travel loose in the car, as it could easily be thrown about. A puppy should get used to its box at home, to the point where it is regarded as a haven. Never shut the dog in a box as a punishment. The wooden show boxes that are most commonly used are not available in pet shops. However, any of the breed club secretaries will be able to put you in touch with someone who makes them to order. They are often on sale at club shows.

FOOD AND EXERCISE

In order to move correctly, the Yorkie, although very small in size, still needs to be well-muscled, with a good, hard body. This is achieved by feeding and exercising the dog correctly, bearing in mind that the health of the coat also is affected by the food that is eaten. Too much red meat can overheat the blood and cause the dog to scratch, so care must be taken in the diet to avoid this while still feeding enough body-building food. During the course of a week, I feed about fifty percent beef mince – either raw or scalded – and fifty percent white meat or fish, which must be cooked through. I mix this with a little biscuit, such as the pin head meal, and I also add a little cooked vegetable in with the food – this is whatever I happen to be cooking for the family that day. My adult dogs are always fed two meals a day: one in the morning and one in the evening.

To develop the muscles correctly, the dog should be road-walked in a fairly flat area. Do not allow it to pull on the lead, as this over-develops the shoulder muscles and results in poor movement. Road-walking should be undertaken for about half-an-hour each day, over and above the normal exercise in the garden. Remember to walk out briskly so that the dog is moving with its head up and with purpose.

BASIC OBEDIENCE

It never ceases to amaze me how many people do not think that basic obedience is needed for the show ring. It is absolutely essential from many points of view. If something unforeseen happens and the dog slips its lead, it would create major problems if the dog did not come to your call. At a show there are many hundreds of dogs in a small area, and while you are walking round, a dangerous situation could very quickly develop, unless a dog is obedient to the owner's voice. The lead should never be depended on as the only aid to obedience and control. Yorkies that are not obedient can be really naughty, and I have heard many people say that if it was a large breed, it would be banned from shows. I do not agree with this, because if it was a large breed, owners would be forced to spend much more time on training. The Yorkshire Terrier is a very intelligent breed of dog, and they do not suffer fools gladly. How many times do we see judges hesitating over a particular Yorkie in the ring, going over and over the coat and pulling at the falls? How often do we watch, with baited breath, wondering how the dog will react? Trained show dogs know when enough is enough, and will let the judge know in no uncertain manner. Unfortunately, it is always the dog that gets the blame in this situation, when in actual fact it is the fault of the judge for taking too much time and not making a positive decision – and the fault of the owner for not training the dog to the point where it knows it must never bite a judge, however stupid it feels that the judge is! There are very few Yorkies that are downright vicious; it is up to us to train them to understand what is expected of them – and a little bit more besides.

In whatever situation you are training, be it on the table, out walking, or simply playing in the garden, always aim to train your dog to understand certain words and to respond quickly to the words. 'Leave' is the word that I begin with, and even very young puppies can learn this. If a pup starts to chew a piece of furniture, just say "leave" very firmly, and move it away from the object. You may have to repeat this a number of times before the puppy gets the idea, but it will eventually, and it is a very useful command. Gradually add further words, especially when you are walking the dog, such as 'steady', when it is moving too fast, or 'come on', when it is moving too slowly. The real benefit of these two commands is in the show ring. If you have to tug on the lead to slow the dog down, this will pull it out of stride. Whereas, if you just use your voice, the dog slows down naturally, without any visible sign of the hindquarters being affected, and this allows the judge to assess the movement correctly. Never underestimate the intelligence of dogs; they are capable of learning and responding to many words and commands. It is just a matter of time and patience.

EXHIBITING

This is the culmination of all your hard work: breeding, rearing, training, and grooming. People do come and go in the dog game, but once you have been truly 'bitten by the bug', it becomes a way of life, whether you are very successful or just enjoy taking your dog for a day out. All exhibitors need to plan and prepare for shows in a very methodical manner. Assuming that your dog is now fully trained and you wish to compete in the show ring, the first step is to order one of the dog papers from your newsagent, and these give the dates and details of all the shows. It is a good idea to attend a few shows without taking your dog, especially the club shows that are only for Yorkies. Go along and make yourself known to the secretary, and explain that you are a complete novice and you wish to join the club and learn as much as you can before actually exhibiting your dog. This will give you a good insight into the procedures of the show ring. Watch the dogs being shown, and then talk to the exhibitors afterwards, when they are more relaxed. You will soon find that you have made new friends who are only too willing to help you, and will explain anything that you do not understand. At first the whole business seems very complicated, but familiarity will clarify the picture.

When you decide that both you and your dog are ready to compete, select a show that is not too far from home. Ideally, it should be a small open show with classes for Yorkies. Contact the secretary of the show, and you will be sent a schedule. Read this very carefully, and when you have filled it in, re-read it to make certain that you have not made any mistakes. If you inadvertently state the incorrect birthdate of the dog, or make a mistake with the spelling of its name, it could be disqualified if it wins a prize. Return the completed entry form, with the entry fee, to the secretary, and keep the schedule in a safe place, making a note of the class in which you have entered your dog. I always write the name of the dog that I am taking, and the class, on the front of the schedule. Show equipment should be prepared well in advance of the event.

REQUIREMENTS FOR THE SHOW BOX

1. A clean, pure-bristle brush.
2. A clean, stainless-steel comb.
3. A red show lead. (Any colour is permitted, but it is normally accepted that red is best suited to a Yorkie.)
4. A red box cover – again, any colour is permitted. (A box cover is not required in countries where the Yorkie is shown on the floor.)
5. Rubber-bands.
6. Red ribbon to tie up the topknot. (Any colour permitted.)
7. Clip or safety-pin for the ring number.
8. Spray bottle containing clean water.

9. Scissors – hair-dressing type.
10. Cotton-wool.
11. Eye drops e.g. Optrex.
12. A towel.
13. Almond oil – for after the dog has been shown.
14. Cut and folded acid-free tissue paper.
15. Finger gauze for the boots.
16. Microtape to hold them in place.
17. Disinfectant.
18. Small, portable grooming table.

In addition to the above, I always carry an emergency kit containing antiseptic cream, anti-diarrhoea tablets, and travel sickness tablets. The show box should always be kept entirely separate from the daily grooming box, and the day after the show all the grooming equipment should be washed and replaced ready for the next outing. As well as your grooming equipment, do be sure and take some food, a bottle of water and a bowl, for the dog's needs during the day. It is quite likely that you will be away from home for most of the day. It is a good idea to take a little food for yourself, plus a hot drink in a thermos-flask. Refreshments are available at all shows, but as you must never leave your dog unattended, it is often easier to take your own provisions.

Having prepared everything for the show the night before, plan to leave the house in plenty of time, in order to arrive at least an hour before the judging is due to start. Wear something neat and tidy that will complement the colour of your dog, but at the same time it is important to be comfortable.When you arrive at the show, get settled in an area near to the ring where the Yorkies are scheduled to be judged. If it is a benched show, make sure that you wipe the bench with disinfectant before allowing your dog on it – even if you are using a newspaper and a blanket. Give your dog a drink of water, and then take it for a little walk so that it can relieve itself in the stipulated area. The atmosphere of a show is exciting but often quite noisy, so while you are walking your dog allow it time to adjust to this – let it stand and stare at all the new sights and sounds.

This is the time to set up your table and start grooming the dog ready for the ring. Firstly, remove all the crackers and spray the complete coat with a little water. Do not use too much, only enough to dampen it. Check the eyes and, if necessary, wipe them with a little Optrex on some cotton-wool. Next, brush the coat until it is completely dry, using long, firm strokes in an effort to prevent the coat from waving. Do not be tempted to stop brushing until the coat is dry, or the hair will kink and it will look awful. Once this happens, it is very hard to get the hair straight again without totally re-bathing. After the coat has been brushed dry, take a comb in your right hand and run it through the hair, always combing with your right hand and smoothing the coat down with the palm of your left hand. This is where the art of grooming really comes to the fore: you must not brush or comb the hair for so long that the natural oils make the coat appear greasy, but you must stop at the point where the coat is shining, and lying flat and even over the body. Every texture of coat is different, so it is impossible to calculate exactly how long this process will take. This is where practice makes perfect, and each time that you bath your dog at home, experiment on reaching this point.

The topknot is very important to the finished effect, and so, again, time must be taken at home

INSERTING THE RIBBON

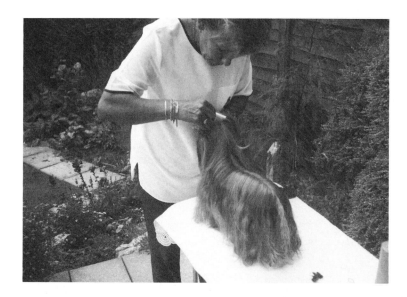

Using a steel comb, make a parting between and slightly behind the ears. Draw the hair forward and hold it in the left hand.

Continue to hold the hair from between the ears in the left hand, and make a parting on both sides of the head, from the corners of the eyes to the middle of the base of the ears. Comb the hair from the skull into the left hand.

Photos: Bob Fisher.

*Hold all the hair from
the head firmly in the
left hand.*

*Insert the rubber
band, ensuring that it
is not too tight.*

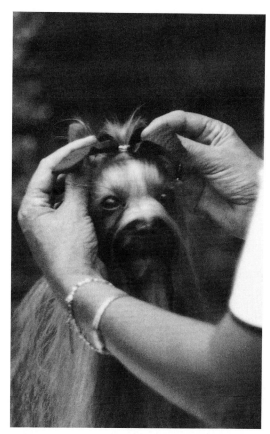

Tie the ribbon over the rubber band; tying a neat bow takes a lot of practice.

Gaysteps Golden Haze at Shianda, complete with ribbon.

to perfect this. Taking the comb, make a parting from the outer corner of the eye in a straight line to the middle of the base of the ear, and comb the hair up into your left hand. Repeat this at the other side, so that all the hair from the skull is in your left hand. Holding this hair firmly, comb the hair from between the ears, taking care not to include the blue coat from the top of the neck. Now you have all the hair that forms the topknot in your left hand. Comb all the hair upwards until it is even, and then wrap a rubber-band around it, aiming to place the band between the ears. Take care not to include any hair from the ear leathers. Now check the placement of the topknot, and ensure that the hair is not pulled too tight so that the eyes look as though they are bulging. Finally, tie a small bow of ribbon around the rubber-band, and neaten it with the scissors.

Make a straight parting down the centre of the back by going to the rear of the dog and brushing the hair straight back from just behind the ears to the tail. Using the comb, part the coat and comb the hair down each side of the body. Put on the lead, and position it under the neck and behind the ears, where it will not interfere with the general outline and lie of the coat. Just before you go into the ring, give the coat a last comb through. Do not wait until you get into the ring to do this, as it is important to make a good first impression on the judge. Remain calm and concentrate on your dog. Do not fuss with it too much; just set the dog up and keep talking to it very quietly. Comb the coat just to arrange it neatly, and then leave the dog alone. So many exhibitors work feverishly on the coat during the whole of the class; this is not only unnecessary, it also spoils the dog's chances of winning. The judge does not want to look at someone's head bent over the dog, or to see the coat flying everywhere as it is vehemently brushed – it ruins the whole picture. When you are asked to put the dog on the table, do so with a minimum of fuss. Stand it up, quickly brush down and tidy the coat, and then stand back to give the judge as much room as possible. When your class has finished, return to your bench, and oil and cracker your dog as quickly as possible to avoid hair breakage. Then take it to the stipulated area so that it can relieve itself.

When you are showing, always comport yourself in a correct manner. There may well come a time when you will feel that the judge has been less than fair with you, but you must take the rough with the smooth, as there will also be times when you win when you thought you were not going to. The dog world is going through very difficult times at the moment and we appear to be getting far more bad publicity than good, so it is up to us to give the best impression that we can to the public to change this situation. Remember to put all rubbish in the bins provided or take it all home with you and dispose of it there. If your dog should defecate while you are away from home, then clean it up and dispose of it in a proper manner.

If you are showing your dog during the summer, then you will need to make provisions for the hot weather, both while travelling and at the show. First and foremost, never leave your dog in the car. Personally, I do not think that a dog should be left unattended in a car in any weather, but it is particularly dangerous in warm weather. When the sun is out it does not take very long for the inside temperature of the car to become unbearable, and the dog will quickly become distressed and death will follow in a very short space of time. While travelling in the heat there are numerous things that can be done to keep your dog comfortable. Non-spill bowls are available at all good pet shops, plus bowls that will hang on the inside of the wire of the show box. Make sure that water is always available, and take a large bottle of water with you. If your dog starts to pant and show signs of distress, then pour some water on to a towel and put it on to the dog, and open all the windows of the car. I take the ice-trays from a picnic basket with me

Ch. Crosspins Royal Brigadier all ready for the show ring.

and wrap them in a towel under the dog, and I put a portable fan in front of the door of the cage, which ensures that the dog stays cool. If all this fails and the dog is in distress, get the dog out of the car as quickly as possible and pour cold water on it, in order to lower its temperature. Do not attempt to continue your journey until the weather is cooler and the dog has fully recovered.

Showing dogs is a wonderful sport for people of any age; it can be undertaken as little or as often as you like. I have written here about the strict routine of grooming and crackering a Yorkie, but this does not mean that if you do not adhere to this regime, you cannot show your dog. On the contrary, providing that the registration regulations of the Kennel Club are met, any dog can be shown – good, bad or indifferent. There are many small shows that you and your dog can attend and enjoy, and as long as you realise that your dog is not top show-quality, or that it lacks coat because you do not wish to cracker, then I say, go and try it. You will enjoy meeting new friends and the social atmosphere, and if you are on your own, it is one of the hobbies that will ensure that you will not be alone for long.

Chapter Thirteen

JUDGING

In this chapter I am not attempting to explain what to look for in a Yorkie – I have done that in my interpretation of the Breed Standard – but if you have accepted a judging appointment you should know what to look for; if you do not, then you should not be judging. This chapter is purely for the novice judge, to help them with the technical aspects of judging and the code of ethics. To be asked to judge is an honour; it is also a great responsibility and should not be undertaken lightly. Usually people are not invited to judge until they have been showing dogs for about five years, starting with small shows and graduating to Championship level. We all know that some people accept appointments before this, but to be able to go into a ring with the complete confidence that you know your breed, will certainly reflect in your judging. I personally believe that before anyone is allowed to judge, they should have spent some time stewarding, which gives the groundwork to ring procedure and an insight into judging, before taking on the actual task.

The night before you are due to judge, make sure that everything that you will need is ready, so that you are not rushing around at the last minute. It is a good idea to read through the Breed Standard to put yourself in the right frame of mind and to collect your thoughts. Dress sensibly both for the judging and the weather; there is nothing worse than wearing thin summer clothes and trying to judge when you are freezing cold. On the morning of the show, set off from home in plenty of time to allow yourself to reach the show at least an hour before judging is due to start, so that when you arrive, there will be time to make yourself known to the secretary and have some refreshment. It is amazing how much you will appreciate those few minutes before you are called to the ring. Acquaint yourself with the steward, and remember that he or she will have quite an amount of work to do in order for your judging to run smoothly, so give the instructions as to how you want the ring conducted, placement of new dogs etc., in a polite and friendly manner. There is no excuse for judges bullying the stewards.

When all is prepared, ask the steward to call the first class into the ring. Watch the dogs as they enter, for you are judging the dogs from the moment they enter the ring to the moment that they leave it; use every second available to make mental notes. Give the exhibitors plenty of time to get their dogs settled before you walk the length of the line-up, approaching each dog from the front, then viewing the side, and lastly the hindquarters. I never touch a dog at this point, I just

Anne Fisher judging in Germany.

look, making mental notes of each exhibit. Then invite the first person in the line-up to put their dog on the table for you to examine. It is not important in what order you go over each point of the dog, but it is advisable to always use the same method, so that you don't inadvertently miss a point. I will describe the order that I use, but it is entirely up to you. The only point I would make is that, under no circumstances, should a dog be approached from behind. This could startle it, and put him off for the duration of the class.

Approach the front of the dog in a confident and purposeful manner, without being overbearing. You can offer the back of your hand for the dog to sniff, but do not twiddle your fingers about. Take the head in your hands, taking note of eyes, skull, muzzle and nose; examine the teeth and jaw, and check the ear placement to ascertain that the ears are not tied up into the ribbon. Look at the ear leathers – do they have hair on them or are they bald and black, suggesting stripped ear? Run your thumb from the base of the stop to between the ears in order to confirm that the dog has a moderate stop and a flat skull. Examine for the shading and clearing of the tan from the roots of the hair on the skull and on the sides of the face and muzzle. While you are still standing at the front of the dog, use both hands to gently lift the front, and allow the feet and legs to take up a natural stance on the table. Run a hand down each shoulder and down the leg to make sure that the dog is not out at elbow and that the front legs are straight. Then pick one foot up at a time to see if the feet are round and the toenails black.

Move to the side of the dog, and note the length of neck. Place the thumb and forefinger of your right hand on the points of the shoulder blades, and trace the outline of the shoulder blade with your left hand. Are the shoulders well laid, or is the dog straight in shoulder? Are the front legs straight when viewed from the side, with the paws in a direct line underneath the points of the shoulders? I prefer to set the dog up myself on the table when I examine the topline; it gives me the 'feel' of the dog. Run your fingers along the spine – this is the only way to be sure of the

Ch. Chantmarles Dolly Dimple (UK): top Yorkie in 1979 and Best of Breed, Crufts 1980.

topline, and to find out whether there are any deformities. The Breed Standard states that the Yorkie should have a moderate spring of rib, and this is very important – especially so with bitches. Go over the ribs, proceeding along the body to ascertain the amount of body weight carried.

When examining the tail-set, gently lift the tail and note whether it appears to be a continuation of the spine, or is too low or too high-set, and if so, why? Separate the coat on the hindquarters so that you can see clearly the turn of stifle, checking that there is no exaggeration, and whether the feet are pointing forward, with no evidence of cow hocks. Move to the back of the dog so that you can see the hindquarters straight on. Are the hindlegs straight and well-muscled, and placed directly under the body? If you are examining a male animal, check that both testicles are descended into the scrotum. Now gently lift the hindquarters just off the table, and test if the hindlegs are sound, with no clicking that could indicate slipping patellas.

As you can see, I have moved from the head of the dog to the tail, examining only the structure and soundness of the dog, apart from the colour on the face and head. Now is the time to judge the colour and texture of the entire coat, bearing in mind that there are two sides to a dog. Take the brush from the exhibitor, and move again to the front of the dog. Brush and separate the coat, in order to view the colour on the chest and front legs. Always check from the roots of the hair to the tips, noting colour, shading and texture. Proceed to the side of the dog and, using the same method of brushing and separating the coat, check for colour-run behind the head at the top of the neck, above the elbows on the front legs, and above the stifles on the hindquarters. Has the tan run into the blue along the body or above the tail? Is the blue a lot lighter on the tail, indicating a going-over of colour? The back coat of the Yorkie should be an even, dark steel-blue, and if you are in any doubt because of bad lighting, do not hesitate to take the dog nearer to a window or doorway. You are there to judge the dog to the best of your ability, and you cannot do that if it is not possible to see properly – in some halls the lighting completely distorts the colour. While you have been brushing and separating the coat, you should be taking note of the texture at the same time as looking at colour and shading. However, in order to get the true picture of the texture, lift the coat with the brush and let it fall naturally. A soft coat will not fall back into place in the same way as a correct silk coat, and your experience will now really come into play with the actual feel of the coat.

After completing your examination of the dog on the table, ask the exhibitor to move it up and down on the mat, twice. If the ring is very large, or you are judging outside, you can ask the handler to move the dog in a triangle first. Whichever method you use, the important thing is for you to be able to assess the movement – going away from you for the hindquarters, coming towards you for the forequarters – plus the side view for the topline and carriage. When you are satisfied that your assessment of the dog is complete, thank the exhibitor. If you have a very large class and you feel that you will not be able to remember the good and bad points of each dog, then return to the table and make a few notes in your judging book – this is infinitely better than making a diabolical mistake. Move on to your next exhibit, repeating the procedure until you have 'seen' all the dogs.

A mistake that a number of judges make in subsequent classes is to forget the dogs that are in the ring from previous classes. One way to avoid this is to ask the steward to move these dogs to the end of the current line-up, as soon as you have seen the last dog. When selecting your winners, do not appear hesitant: it gives a bad impression, appearing as though you don't know what you are doing. There was never a saying more applicable than 'He who hesitates is lost'. Of course, there is always the occasion when you have two dogs of very similar quality and you want to compare them, but this is very different from wandering aimlessly up and down the line-up. Bring your winners to the centre of the ring and dismiss the rest of the class by thanking them.

The ability to judge well and honestly is imperative for the future of the breed, and it will gain you respect within the breed. At times you will have to be very single-minded, especially when you have a friend in the class, who may have a rather mediocre dog. Yes, you could give that dog a first prize, but who loses? You do, because you have made a fool of yourself in front of many exhibitors, who know exactly what you are doing. There will be moments in your judging career when you will come under all kinds of different pressures – unfortunately there are always the odd ones in any group that think that they can make their own rules. The pressure comes in many different guises, and it never ceases to amaze me that these people truly believe that you don't realise what they are doing. Like the 'friend' who rang me the night before I was due to judge, with the excuse that he wanted to know the way to the show. This man had been showing regularly for over twenty years, and the directions were very clear in the schedule. On the day, his dog did not merit more than a fourth place, which is what I gave him!

Do not be intimidated by the top breeders; they do not always have the best dog present. Equally, do not intimidate the novice exhibitors; they represent the future of our breed. The aim

Ch. Status Quo at Beechrise (left) Best of Breed Crufts 1992, owned by Hilda Griffiths, and Ch. Clantalon Credentials, Reserve CC, owned by Mr and Mrs Douglas McKay. Judge George Down.

is to be able to walk away from the ring having done the job to the best of your ability. In other words, be prepared for some aggravation – it goes with the job. Judging will teach you a tremendous amount about the different lines in our breed, the prevalent faults and the dominant virtues, but as a judge, you must never be tempted to discuss a particular dog with anyone but the owner. You are there to judge the dogs as a representative of your Kennel Club; it is a position of honour, so do not abuse that trust.

Chapter Fourteen

GENERAL HEALTH CARE

Yorkshire Terriers are, on the whole, a hardy breed, but all owners should be able to take a dog's temperature and should be aware of the symptoms of the most common diseases. Prevention is always better than cure, and there are numerous ways in which you can help your dog to stay healthy. In this chapter I have highlighted the most common ailments, but if you are ever worried about your dog's health, do not hesitate to contact your vet immediately. Keep a first-aid kit in the house for emergencies. This should contain:

1. An anal thermometer: this can be purchased at a chemist's, but be sure to ask for the anal thermometer, which has a smaller, thicker bulb of mercury at its base than an oral thermometer. There are now digital thermometers available which are very simple to use.
2. Vaseline: to lubricate the thermometer.
3. Antiseptic solution: such as TCP, for cleaning wounds.
4. Antiseptic cream: for dressing wounds.
5. Bandages.
6. Micropore tape: to secure the bandages.
7. Anti-diarrhoeal medicine: Kaolin (for children) is excellent for treating simple diarrhoea.
8. Cotton-wool.
9. Tweezers: for removing grass seeds or bee stings.
10. Scissors.
11. Eye wash: such as Optrex.

TAKING THE TEMPERATURE
If your dog appears listless and unwell, and its nose is dry and warm – even when the dog is moving about – you should take its temperature. However, you should bear in mind that a dog's nose can be dry and a little warm when it is resting or asleep, and this is perfectly normal. It is a good idea to ask a helper to hold the dog for you, until you become experienced in taking the temperature. The best method is to place the thermometer in your right hand and dip the base of it into the Vaseline. Then, with your left hand, lift the tail and insert the thermometer gently into the anus, going in about an inch, and hold it there for about one minute before withdrawing it.

Ch. Chantmarles Best Intentions (UK). (Int. Ch. Ozmilion Jubilation – Ch. Chantmarles Dolly Dimple). Bred by Mary Hayes. Yorkies are a hardy breed, and should hopefully live a long and healthy life.

The normal temperature for a dog is 101.5 Fahrenheit, and more than a degree either way indicates that the dog is unwell and must be attended to.

DIRTY BOTTOMS

It might surprise you to find this topic in a chapter on general health, but I have included it here because many new owners of Yorkies think that the puppy is ill, judging by its appearance and actions, when in actual fact it just has a dirty bottom. There are times when faeces get caught on the coat, and when this happens, the Yorkie takes up a very typical stance. It will crouch over and be very unwilling to move, look thoroughly miserable as though it is not at all well. Once you have seen this stance, you will always be able to recognise what the problem is. However, the first time you see it, it can be quite a shock, so it is as well to check your dog each time that it relieves itself.

Mrs Betty Whitbread, of the Brybett prefix, recalls that she was not informed of this problem when she bought her first Yorkie, and when the puppy got a dirty bottom she did not, at first, realise what was wrong. She was really worried, thinking that the dog was ill, and when she did realise, she was then horrified that she had got to wash a dirty bottom. Now she instils it into all potential owners that some areas of owning a Yorkie are definitely not as pleasant as others, and if you are not prepared to perform this task, then a Yorkie is not the breed for you. I am sure that every Yorkie breeder in the world would second this.

INOCULATIONS

It is crucial to have your dog vaccinated against a number of diseases. The first course is usually given at about ten weeks of age, and it consists of two injections containing a number of vaccines which are administered with a two week interval between the first and the second injection. Subsequently the dog will need a booster every year. This booster is of equal importance to the original course; it does exactly what it says and boosts the antibodies back to a safe level. Many people are under the mistaken impression that after the first course of vaccines the dog does not really require any more. This is totally untrue, and what they are actually doing is relying on everyone else having their dogs vaccinated. These inoculations are to prevent killer diseases, and if the dog is not inoculated and contracts one of these diseases, it can die a most painful death. This can be prevented by taking your dog to the vet just once a year, and surely that is worth anything. Although the first course of injections is usually started at ten weeks, this can differ slightly according to the time of year and whether there is a lot of disease reported in the area. At times, puppies will require a parvovirus inoculation at a much earlier age; no puppy should be sold and go to a new environment without the parvo jab. The antibodies from the mother are passed on to the puppy, so if the puppy has been hand-reared, or if the mother has not been inoculated, the parvo-vaccine should be given earlier than usual. Be guided by your vet on this important issue.

DISEASES THAT THE VACCINES GUARD AGAINST
1. Distemper (hard pad).
2. Infectious Canine Hepatitis.
3. Adenovirus.
4. Parvovirus.
5. Parainfluenza.
6. Leptospira canicola
7. Leptospira icterohaemorrhagiae.

WORMS

There are numerous products on the market that will eradicate the two main types of worms that we have in Britain, which are roundworms and tapeworms. In the United States and warmer countries of the globe, heartworms and others types of worm are also a problem. In these countries dogs should be tested and treated by the vet, as should any dog imported into Britain. Puppies must be wormed no later than six weeks of age, and at regular intervals throughout the dog's life, whether symptoms of a worm infestation appear or not. The worming products available are extremely safe; some of them such as Shirley's Worming Cream and Shaw's Erliworm can be administered as early as three weeks of age and can be obtained from pet shops.

Most puppies suffer from roundworms. The symptoms are a bloated stomach, and irregular eating habits – one day eating ravenously and another day hardly eating anything at all. In severe cases creamy-white worms are visible in the stool and the puppy can vomit worms. This will obviously seriously affect the general health of the dog, and with regular worming a dog should never reach this stage of infestation. Particular attention should be paid to the dam, as she will pass the larvae on to her offspring. Once the medication has been administered, the worms will be expelled in the faeces within twenty-four hours, and this should be removed immediately. Tapeworms are more likely to occur in the adult dog. In cases of infestation, creamy-white pieces of the worm, about the size of a grain of rice, will appear around the anus of the dog, and the dog will also have a depraved appetite. As tapeworms are more difficult to eradicate than roundworms, I would advise medication obtained from your vet.

STRIPPED EAR

The ear-leathers of a dog suffering from this condition will be bald inside and out, and will appear crusty, black and oily. The coat on the tail and the hocks is affected as well. No one has really been able to prove what causes this, but there are many theories. Some say that it is caused by a mite under the skin, and others believe that it is the result of blocked oil glands. I have had several tests done on various Yorkies' ears, and none of them have resulted in a positive conclusion. However, if the leathers are kept scrupulously clean and free from oil, by whatever method, it will cure the stripped ear eventually, but it does take several weeks. Each day, carefully wash the ear-leathers with a little mild shampoo and wipe them dry – do not rub, or the ears will become sore and bleed. Take care not to get almond oil on the ears while you are grooming, if you are treating a show dog.
Prevention: Keep the ear-leathers clean and dry and free from oil.

EAR MITE

This is a minute mite, invisible to the human eye, and it is mainly contracted from cats. It causes the dog to scratch its ears, and hold its head on one side. In severe cases, when the ear is touched at the base, it squelches and has a bad odour; the inside of the ear appears inflamed and a dark, waxy substance exudes from it. Veterinary help must be sought. Do not attempt to dig down into the ear to remove the debris, as the inflamed ear canal is very delicate, and you will do more harm than good.
Prevention: Regular cleaning of the ears with a proprietory oil, obtained from pet shops.

EYE INFECTIONS

If the whites of the eyes appear red and sore, or there is excessive mucus in the corners of the eyes, bathe them with an eye wash, such as Optrex, several times a day. If the condition does not improve within a couple of days, or if the dog is trying to rub the eyes, veterinary help must be sought as soon as possible.

DIARRHOEA

This problem should always be taken very seriously, especially if it occurs in young puppies. More often than not, it is simply that the diet has been changed, or the puppy has drunk too much milk. If the stools are loose, but not watery, then a dose of Kaolin – a medicine for children – will quickly cure the problem. Food and milk should be withheld for twenty-four hours, but make sure that water is always available so that the dog does not become dehydrated.

If the onset is sudden, the stools are watery or they contain any blood, the dog must be taken to the vet immediately. Failure to do this could result in death. Once the diarrhoea has been cured, care must be taken with the diet for a few days. Only feed small amounts of easily digestible low-fat foods such as white meat, or fish, or boiled egg mixed in a little boiled rice. Do not offer any milk for a few more days, and only re-introduce it gradually.

CONSTIPATION

If the constipation is severe, the dog will strain to pass a motion, and when it does, it will often cry with pain. The faeces will appear hard and dry, and may even have streaks of blood on where they have scratched the anus or the bowel. Administer a little milk of magnesia or liquid paraffin, and change the diet by adding more roughage, and perhaps a little milk.
Prevention: Give a balanced diet of meat, biscuits and cooked vegetables, adjust the diet as and when necessary, before the constipation becomes severe.

BLOCKED ANAL GLANDS

A dog suffering from this condition will scoot along the floor in a sitting position, and as the condition worsens it will bite itself on the hindquarters, or on top of the back in front of the tail. If left untreated, an abscess will develop on the glands, which are situated on either side of the anus. This condition is very often caused by an incorrect diet, lacking in roughage – although some dogs are more prone to it than others. When the fluid is secreted from the anal glands, it has a foul odour. The best time to relieve this condition is when you are bathing the dog. Take a piece of old towelling, soak it in warm water, and hold it to the anal glands for a minute or so. Then, with the towel still over the anus, use your thumb and forefinger to squeeze each side, and behind the anus, and this will express the fluid. If the anal glands have abscessed, do not attempt to treat the dog. You will need to go the vet, who will administer antibiotics and give instructions on how to clean the glands.
Prevention: Add more roughage to the diet, and clean the anal glands as soon as you observe any of the symptoms. Some breeders advocate cleaning the anal glands as part of the general routine. Personally, I do not favour this, because Yorkies are not normally prone to anal gland problems, and the more often they are emptied by the owner, the less likely they are to continue working naturally on their own. I prefer to feed a correct diet with plenty of roughage, and only resort to emptying the glands when I feel that it is necessary.

FLEAS

These can be an absolute menace. They are most active during the summer months; if they are not treated they will quickly multiply and get into the soft furnishing, such as carpets and furniture. Fleas are reddish-brown in colour, and they prefer the warmest areas of the animal – under the neck, tops of the legs and the belly. When the coat of the dog is parted, they may be visible to the human eye scuttling over the body, but more often the first signs are the flea excreta, which looks like small particles of grit. Because Yorkies are close to the ground and have long coats, they can easily pick up fleas any time that they are out walking. If, by any chance you have a hedgehog in your garden, try to remove it, as hedgehogs are normally full of fleas. The dog should be bathed regularly, using an anti-flea shampoo, and it should be sprayed, using a product such as Nuvantop, which can be obtained from your vet. If a dog has been infested with fleas, all its bedding should be renewed. Should the fleas get into the soft furnishings, these will also have to be treated, using a spray especially manufactured for furniture, in order to eradicate them.

LICE
These are much smaller than fleas and are creamy-grey in colour. They are eradicated in the same way as fleas.

TICKS
These are parasites that live on the blood of warm-blooded animals, burying their heads underneath the skin of the animal in order to do this. They are most commonly found in an area where sheep graze, but they can also be found just about anywhere. They are visible to the human eye, and are grey in colour. Once a tick has attached itself to a dog, it does not move, but it grows larger as it ingests more blood. Do not attempt to remove the tick by pulling it, as the head will be left under the skin of the dog, and will become infected. One method is to paint the tick all over with nail varnish; this will kill it, and so it will release its hold without any harm to the dog.

RINGWORM
This is contagious, both to humans and to dogs. It can be picked up anywhere from other animals, but it is most commonly caught in areas where cattle are grazing. An infected dog will start to scratch, and bald, round patches will appear on the body. The edges of these will be reddened and slightly rough. The dog should be isolated from other dogs, and the owner should wear thin hospital-type rubber gloves when handling the animal. Veterinary assistance should be sought. Ringworm is much more easily cured now than it used to be, and a course of tablets and ointment for the affected patches will soon clear up the problem once it has been diagnosed.

BEE STINGS
During the summer when there are a lot of bees about, a dog can easily get stung, especially if it insists on chasing them, as some do. If the dog is stung in the mouth, you must seek veterinary help at once, in case the throat swells and closes. Otherwise, try to remove the sting with a pair of tweezers and apply antiseptic cream to the area. Observe the dog closely, and if there is any sign that the dog is in distress, seek veterinary help.

GRASS SEEDS
From the middle to the end of the summer, grass seeds can be a real danger to dogs. They will pierce the skin and if they are not removed promptly, they will enter the body, more often than not getting between the toes and into the ears. Each time that you return from exercising your dog, check to see if it has picked up any seeds, and if so, remove them immediately. If they have already pierced the skin, remove them with a pair of tweezers and bathe the area with an antiseptic solution, and then apply antiseptic cream. Try to keep the grass in your garden short.

INGUINAL HERNIA
Occasionally, a puppy may be born with a lump in the groin; it may not be noticed until the puppy starts to become really active. Very often vets will not operate to repair the hernia until the dog is over twelve months of age, unless it is causing discomfort or there is a fear of it

strangulating. In some cases when Yorkies are born with inguinal hernias, it can happen that as the puppy grows and becomes stronger, the hernia can entirely disappear. However, if it does not, then I would definitely advise surgery. Never mate a bitch which has a hernia of this type, as in the early weeks of pregnancy a whelp could become lodged in it, and this could kill the bitch.

UMBILICAL HERNIA

Again, this can be congenital, but can be worsened, or even caused, by the mother of the puppy when she tries to sever the cord at birth and pulls too hard. Some breeders bind the part of the body where the hernia is located in an attempt to allow it to repair itself. I have never known this method to work, although I have been assured that it can. In my experience, the hernia either stays the same size as the puppy grows, and so appears smaller in comparison to the body, or it gets larger. This type of hernia should be operated on as soon as the vet is willing to perform the operation, to avoid any complications occurring.

LUXATING PATELLAS

This is often referred to as slipping stifles, and it occurs when the knee-cap, which is situated on the stifle, slips to either side. This condition is hereditary, but it can also be caused by injury, or by excessive exercise at too young an age – especially with toy breeds such as the Yorkie. Puppies should not be allowed to have too much exercise, and their exercise should always be supervised. They should not be permitted to chase round like hooligans until they are exhausted, or to jump from one piece of furniture to the next. It is important to allow the bones to grow and the muscles to develop naturally and normally. When a dog has luxating patellas, it will hold one leg up intermittently. As the condition worsens the legs will appear bowed, and finally the patella may not return to its correct position. If the condition becomes severe, then surgery will be necessary, but as soon as any lameness is noticed a vet must be consulted, who will advise you from the onset of the condition.

PERTHES DISEASE

This is an hereditary disease; the blood supply is cut off from the head of the femur in the hind leg, causing the head of the bone to die. It manifests itself at about seven to ten months of age when the puppy will appear lame, trying to walk with its weight on its front legs. As soon as any lameness is observed, the dog should be taken to the vet. Although Perthes is hereditary, a similar condition can be caused by injury. Many years ago, one of my puppies was playing in the kitchen, chasing round as puppies will. The floor was covered in linoleum, and she was going so fast that she lost her footing and slid with a bang into the skirting boards. I took her to the vet immediately, who confirmed that luckily nothing was broken. However, he warned me that she had taken the full force of the knock on one back leg, and so she should be confined for a period of time until the bruising had subsided. As the weeks went by and the puppy was allowed more freedom, I noticed that she appeared a little bent over and was putting more weight on to her front legs than her back. We returned to the vet, who diagnosed that part of the head of the femur had died due to injury to the blood vessels feeding it. After many weeks of treatment and confinement, the puppy recovered, and although one leg was slightly shorter than the other, she was able to lead a perfectly normal life. This story shows just how easily accidents happen – with dire results. My puppy was very lucky; it could have been a lot worse.

HIP DYSPLASIA

This is hereditary, and is more common in the larger breeds of dog than in the Yorkie. It is a condition that affects growing hips, and is worsened by a puppy being allowed too much exercise. Often the first outward sign is when a dog has trouble getting from the lying position to the standing position; it will labour over the movement and appear to be in pain. The vet's advice must be sought as soon as any difficulty in movement is observed.

Chapter Fifteen

YORKIE RE-HOMING

There are numerous reasons why a Yorkie may need to be re-homed during the course of its life: the owner may die, without making provision for it, or sometimes owners are forced, through no fault of their own, to move to accommodation that will not be suitable for dogs. The reasons are too many to mention, and are not necessarily those that immediately spring to mind when the word 'rescue' is used, such as an animal being badly treated, thrown out of its home to fend for itself, or just no longer wanted. For the purpose of this book, I felt that I needed to do more research into the subject, and so I have spent some time in the company of Mrs Evans, who is in charge of the Yorkshire Terrier Club Re-Homing. She is a fascinating lady, typical of people throughout the world who dedicate themselves to the welfare of their own chosen breed.

Many people are under the illusion that we have very few problems with Yorkies needing re-homing. Comparatively speaking, this is true. Obviously, the larger breeds are much more problematical because of their physical size, but numerically ours is one of the largest breeds, and so that brings its own problems. In an ideal world, any owner who is experiencing difficulties and needs to have their pet re-homed, should go back to the breeder, who in turn should find a good home for it. However, we do not live in an ideal world, as we are all fully aware, and while most reputable breeders will take their puppies back, and indeed, would prefer that the puppies were returned rather than going to an unknown home, we will always have the indiscriminate breeders that are breeding purely for money and do not care what happens to their puppies once they have been sold. This type of breeder considers the Yorkie to be an ideal dog for their purposes, for they are small in size and always in demand. Consequently, this is the source of many of the Yorkies that needing re-homing.

The more that I talked to Mrs Evans, the more I realised just how much behind-the-scenes work is involved in order to make the re-homing schemes run as smoothly and as professionally as they do. Financially, every scheme must be self-sufficient with enough funds to cover every eventuality, and so jumble sales, bring-and-buy stalls, car boot sales and other events are organised to boost the kitty. These all depend on volunteers, such as one lady who collects old leads from her friends and colleagues, another who knits items to be sold on the stall, various others who bake cakes to be sold. Vets are approached to give a reduction in their prices – and veterinary services can be a huge area of expenditure for the scheme, with inoculations needed

Bonnie: happy and contented in her new home.

By kind permission of the Y.T.C. Re-Homing Scheme.

and sometimes expensive treatment required for accident victims. One Yorkie, called Arney, was suspected of being used for dog fighting, and he virtually had to be sewn back together again. The poor little soul was lucky to survive – fortunately he has now been re-homed with loving and caring people. Dogs often have to be collected from long distances, which involves considerable expense, and frequently it is not just inoculations that are required. If the dog has been badly neglected it may have internal and external parasites, or a contagious illness which has to be treated immediately in order to restore the dog to full health. In order to protect the other animals, an isolation kennel must be available.

The people who organise the schemes must, of necessity, be a special kind of person – someone who can control their feelings under the greatest provocation – because it is imperative that there are no recriminations on the owner. The Yorkie is the first, middle and last concern; the scheme would fail if there was any suspicion that proceedings could follow. I was horrified to think that someone could harm a Yorkie to the point of death, and then calmly walk into a re-homing scheme and just leave the dog. Mrs Evans explained that the exception would be if there was any suspicion of organised dog fighting – then action would be taken promptly. But primarily, the aim of the scheme is to take in any Yorkie that is homeless, or in any kind of distress, whatever the circumstances. It is important to remember that owners who are

Bobby: now the beloved pet of the residents at a home for the elderly.
By kind permission of the Y.T.C. Re-homing Scheme.

deliberately cruel are in the minority; far more often Yorkies are neglected through ignorance, and the majority need re-homing because of a genuine change of circumstances. None are turned away.

When owners pass their dogs to the scheme to be re-homed they must fill out a form and sign it. This contains questions that will be helpful in trying to find the most suitable home – such as: Does the dog like children? Is it house trained? Is it lead trained? Can it can be left for short periods of time? The form includes a statement giving full ownership and responsibility for the dog to the Yorkshire Terrier Rescue, and the owners are asked to donate a little money towards the dog's care while it is in a 'foster' home, awaiting adoption. During this time the Yorkie will lead as normal a life as possible, preferably with a family who will love and care for it while it is either recovering – mentally or physically – or being assessed ready for its new home. Each dog has its own file, with all the information and facts that are available recorded in it, and once a Yorkie is registered with the scheme, it remains under the ownership of the scheme for the rest of its life. This provides a safeguard if the new home is found to be unsuitable, or if circumstances change for the new owner – the Yorkie can always be returned to the scheme.

The only reward that the volunteers receive or want, is to see one of their charges go to a new home and be happy; so the prospective owners must be carefully assessed. Many are turned away because they are unsuitable; it could be that the prospective owner is away from home too many hours in a day, or does not possess the necessary understanding to adopt a rescued animal, or many other reasons too numerous to mention. As soon as a prospective owner contacts the re-homing scheme they are sent a form to be completed, giving all the details concerning their family and home environment, and their hopes and intentions for the new member of the family. They must be willing for a representative to call to view the prospective home, and to interview the whole family. If a Yorkie is allocated, the family must consent to annual follow-up visits, to see how the dog is getting along.

Occasionally, a Yorkie may be able to be re-homed very quickly, especially if it has come to the scheme because of the death of its owner. In these cases there are no physical scars and few mental problems. The dog may be confused, but it has no deep-seated problems; the quicker that it can be re-homed and take up a normal life again, the better. Other Yorkies are not so lucky and face many months recovering from their ordeals; but we are lucky that our chosen breed is resilient and courageous – they will fight for their lives to the very last breath.

While I was finding out more about the re-homing scheme I saw some photographs of dogs that had been cruelly treated, taken when they first arrived, and they would make the hardest of people cry. The haunted look in the eyes is apparent in all of them, some with little, wasted bodies, hardly with the energy to stand, others with gaping wounds, so severe that it is a miracle that they recovered. We are known as a nation of dog lovers, but while this is happening in our own backyard, what right have we to judge other countries? The vast majority of neglected dogs originate from puppy farms or pet shops, where care is not taken to vet the new owners as to their suitability to own a dog. It is high time that the government put a stop to this type of trade, so that this source of supply is cut off.

There are many books written on the different breeds of dogs, but few include any information on this shocking subject, and many eyebrows were raised when I insisted on doing so. People have, quite rightly, stated that Yorkies who have been cruelly treated or neglected are only a very small minority of the breed as a whole. I quite agree, but just because they are in the minority does not mean that we can pretend that they do not exist. I wish that there was no necessity for rescue schemes – that would be utopia. However, I feel that all the newcomers to the breed should be made aware of what can happen to puppies if they are placed in unsuitable homes. It is the responsibility of all breeders to do everything in our power to ensure that as few Yorkies have to be re-homed as possible.

The public are now far more aware of the importance of buying a puppy from reputable breeders, rather than from puppy farms or pet shops, and this is largely the result of advertising and campaigning in the press. However, a great deal more work needs to be done in this area. I do not think that a national register is the answer, as in cases of cruelty, all that could be achieved would be the possible conviction of the person after the crime has been committed. Even this would be far from certain, as the register would have the same problem as the defunct dog licence scheme, with only the honest, caring owners registering their dogs.

However, not all is doom and gloom, as I soon learnt when looking through the case histories of various Yorkies. If an elderly Yorkie is admitted into the Yorkshire Terrier Club Re-homing, then nine times out of ten it will be placed with a particular lady who just adores our four-legged pensioners. She knows that they only have a short time to live, and so she loves them even more. How fortunate we are to have someone like this to help. I heard about one Yorkie, called Bobby, who was adopted by a home for the elderly, and he is totally spoilt by all the residents and lives a life of pure luxury. Some of our Yorkies have been adopted by film stars, who have to go through the same formalities as everyone else. Obviously such people could easily afford to buy a Yorkie, but they prefer to provide a good home for a dog that has fallen on hard times.

I have given just a small insight into one particular re-homing scheme, but throughout the UK and in countries all over the world there are many similar organisations, run by dedicated and hard-working people. We must listen to these people, and we must ensure that all newcomers to the breed, and members of breed clubs are made aware of this side of the dog world. With a little thought, so much more could be achieved. What is the point of national registrations, dog wardens and legislation, if the general public have not been educated in the first place?

Chapter Sixteen
BRITISH CHAMPIONS
1947-1992

YEAR/NAME	SEX	0WNER
1947		
Bens Blue Pride	D	Mr Williamson.
Lady Nada	B	Mrs Hebson.
1948		
Hebsonian Jealousy	B	Mrs Hebson.
Weeplustoo of Achmonie	B	Miss Macdonald.
Starlight	D	Mrs Hargreaves.
1949		
Wee Don of Atherleigh	D	Mr Hayes.
McCay of Achmonie	D	Miss Macdonald.
Splendour of Invincia	D	Mrs Swan.
Vemair Parkview Preview	D	Mrs Mair.
Tufty of Johnstounburn	B	Mrs Crookshank.
1950		
Blue Dolly	B	Mr Coates.
Mr. Pim of Johnstounburn	D	Mrs Crookshank.
Dinah Beau	B	Miss Hartley.
Winpal Arine	B	Miss Palmer.
1951		
Wee Gertrude	B	Mrs Chard & Miss Fairchild
Feona of Phylreyne	B	Mrs Raine.
Vemair Principal Boy	D	Mrs Mair.
Sorreldene Honey Son of the Vale	D	Mrs Bradley.
Hopwood Camelia	B	Miss Martin.
Wee Blue Atom	D	Mrs Overett.
Martynwyns Golden Girl	B	Mrs Montgomery.

Martynwyns Surprise of Atherleigh	D	Mr Coates.
1952		
Adora of Invincia	B	Mrs Swan.
Tatania of Invincia	B	Mrs Stirk.
Sunstar of Invincia	D	Mrs Swan.
Blue Bell	B	Miss Noakes.
Someone of Achmoni	D	Miss Macdonald.
Wee Eve of Yadnum	B	Mrs Munday.
Kelsboro Quality Boy	D	Mrs Cross.
Firhill Fairy	B	Mrs Pannett.
Winpal Henrietta	B	Miss Palmer.
Jacaranda Beauty	B	Mrs Montgomery.
1953		
Vemair Spider	D	Mrs Mair.
Martynwyns Debonaire	D	Mr Coates.
Medium of Johnstounburn	B	Mrs Crookshank.
Aerial of Winpal	B	Miss Palmer.
Eoforwic Envoy of Yadnum	D	Mrs Munday.
Jessica of Westridge	B	Mr Grist.
Stirkean Chota Sahib	D	Mrs Stirk.
Butibel Perseus	D	Mrs Russell.
1954		
Midnight Gold of Yadnum	D	Mrs Munday.
Myrtle of Johnstounburn	B	Mrs Crookshank.
Faye of Phylreyne	B	Mrs Raine.
1955		
Burghwallis Little Nip	D	Mrs Betton.
Sehow Independent	B	Miss Howes.
Wadeholme Little Mitzi	B	Mrs Wade.
Stirkean Kandy Boy	D	Mrs Stirk.
Martynwyns Adora	B	Mrs Seymour.
Epperstone Bon Ton	D	Mrs Hill.
Vemair Uncle Sam	D	Mrs Mair.
Eastgrove Gay Boy	D	Mrs Hargreaves.
Delia of Erlcour	B	Mrs Batsford.
Blue Symon	D	Mrs John.
1956		
Pipit of Johnstounburn	B	Mrs Crookshank.
Burantheas Angel Bright	B	Mrs Burfield.
Hilaire of Pookshill	D	Mrs Wood.
Moon Glow of Yadnum	D	Mrs Munday.
Aureola of Winpal	B	Miss Palmer.
1957		
Cressida of Erlcour	B	Mrs Batsford.
Martini	D	Mrs Beech.

Blue Orchid of Hilfore	B	Mrs Seymour.
Prim of Johnstounburn	B	Mrs Rossiter.
Pimbron of Johnstounburn	D	Mrs Crookshank.
Symons Querida of Tolestar	B	Mrs Tole.

1958

Bystander's Replica	D	Miss Logan.
Coulgorm Chloe	B	Mrs C. Hutchin.
Deebees Stirkeans Faustina	B	Mrs Beech.
June's Boy	D	Mr Latliff.
Ravelin Gaiety Boy	D	Miss Noakes.
Sir Lancelot of Astolat	D	Mrs P. Charlton Haw.
Societyrow Dog Friday	D	Mr & Mrs Barrs.
Stirkean's Rhapsody	D	Mrs E. Stirk.

1959

Buranthea's Doutelle	D	Mrs Burfield.
Don Carlos of Progresso	D	Mrs C. Hutchin.
Elaine of Astolat	B	Mrs P. Charlton Haw.
Pagnell Prima Donna of Wiske	B	Mrs K. M. Renton.
Pedimins Piper	D	Mr G. Porter.
Stirkean's Astonoff Horatio	D	Mrs E. Stirk.

1960

Deebees Campari	D	Mrs D. Beech.
Burghwallis Vikki	D	Mrs M. Betton.
Hampark Dandy	D	Mr W. Wilkinson.
My Sweet Susanne	B	Mrs D. Baynes.
Sungold of Supreme	B	Mr D. A. Smith.
Wadeholme Happy Quest	D	Mrs L. J. Wade.

1961

Adora Junior of Hilfore	B	Mr H. D. Seymour.
Burghwallis Brideen	B	Mrs M. Betton.
Deebees Isa La Bella	B	Mrs D. Beech.
Doone of Wiske	B	Mrs K. M. Renton.
Fuchsia of Fiskerton	B	Mrs V. Moyes.
Glamour Boy of Glengonner	D	Mr D. A. Peck.
Leyham Mascot	D	Mrs D. Meyell.
Mamma's Little Topper	D	Mrs K. H. Cherryholme.
Progress of Progresso	D	Mrs C. Hutchins.
Stirkean's Puff Puffin	B	Mrs E. A. Stirk.

1962

Deebees Hot Toddy	D	Mrs D. Beech.
Elmslade Galahad of Yadnum	D	Mrs E. Munday.
Guyton's Spring Blossom	B	Mr G. Kniveton.
Jacaranda Blue Mischief	B	Mrs J. Montgomery.
Kelsbro Blue Pete	D	Mr H. Cross.
Melody Maker of Embyll	B	Mrs C. Hutchin.

Pontana Prodigy Dainty	B	Mr G. Howells.
Stirkean's Mr Tims	D	Mrs E. Stirk.
Sundance of Wiske	B	Mrs K.M. Renton.
1963		
Charm of Wadeholme	B	Mrs L. J. Wade.
Deebees Caromia	B	Mrs S. D. Beech.
Hopwood Desireable	D	Mr J. W. Hutchinson.
Pagnell Peter Pan	D	Mrs S. I. Groom.
Tzumiao's Cheetah of Martinez	B	Mrs E. Gilbert.
Wenscoes Wendolene	B	Miss W. A. Schofield.
Yorkfold Wrupert Bear	D	Mrs D. Rossiter.
1964		
Burantheas Saint Malachy	D	Mrs H. D. Burfield.
Deebees Little Dodo	B	Mrs S. D. Beech.
Goodiff Blue Dragon	D	Mr G. Crowther.
Millfield Mandy	B	Mrs M. Hepworth.
Minerva of Johnstounburn	B	Mrs M. D. Lowrie.
Phirno Magic Moment	B	Miss P. Noakes.
Progresso Lover Boy	D	Mrs C. Hutchin.
Romance of Wiske	B	Mrs K. M. Renton.
Skyrona Blue Prince	D	Mrs G. Sykes.
Yorkfold McPickle	D	Mrs D. Rossiter.
Golden Buttons of Yadnum	B	Mrs E. Munday.
1965		
Anston Cindy Loo	B	Mrs Moore.
My Precious Joss	D	Mrs C. Flockhart.
Ruswel Chorus Girl of Brendali	B	Mrs R. Marshall.
Templevale Niaissmo of Wiske	B	Mrs K.M.Renton.
Viada Rosina	B	Mrs V. A. Monger.
Wedgwood Starmist	D	Mrs M. Logue.
Whisperdales Phirno Carmen	B	Mr R. Wardill.
1966		
Carlwyns Wee Teddy Toff	D	Mrs W. E.Nichols.
Phirno St. George	D	Miss P. Noakes.
Skyrona Blue Girl	B	Mrs G. Sykes.
Templevale Jessica of Wiske	B	Mrs K. M. Renton.
Beechrise Superb	D	Mrs H. Griffiths.
Dorrit's Leyham Scampie	D	Mrs D. Baynes.
Progresso Pearl	B	Mrs C. Hutchin.
Lillyhill Pimbronette	B	Mrs W. Wilson.
Stirkeans Reenie	B	Mrs E. Stirk.
Progresso Prospect	D	Mrs C. Hutchin.
1967		
Buranthea's Luscious Lady	B	Mrs H. D. Burfield.
Blairsville Tinkerbell	B	Mr & Mrs B. Lister.

1969: Ch. Chantmarles Snuff Box (Macstrouds Whitecross Dandini – Mycariad Stargazer). Owned and bred by Mary Hayes.

Pearce.

Dorrit's Susanne's Treasure	B	Mrs D. Baynes.
Heavenly Blue of Wiske	D	Mr & Mrs L. F. Palframan.
Skyrona Blue Bobby of Streamglen	D	Mrs M. Waldram.
Macstroud's Sir Gay.	D	Mr D. Stroud.
Blue Flash of Streamglen	D	Mrs M. Waldram.
Pagnell Blue Peter	D	Mrs S. I. Groom.
Anston Lucy Locket	B	Mrs Moore.
Stirkean's Gerrard's Little Guy	D	Mrs E. Stirk.
1968		
Blairsville Boy Wonder	D	Mr B. Lister.
Chantmarles Mycariad Wild Silk	B	Mrs M. Hayes.
Dandini Jim	D	Mr A. Blamires.
Deebees Doncella	B	Mrs D. Beech.
Luna Star of Yadnum	D	Mrs E. Munday.
Murose Storm	D	Mrs E. Burton.
Tolcarne Brandy Soda	D	Mrs O. Wood.
Whisperdales Temujin	D	Mr R. Wardill.
1969		
Bobby of Beachdal	D	Mrs A. M. Beach.
Chantmarles Snuff Box	B	Mrs M. Hayes.

1972: Ch. Murose Exquisite (Ch. Murose Wee Pippa – Murose Delight).
Owned and bred by Mrs E. Burton.

Fall.

Deanchel's Beau Caprice	D	Mrs E. M. Taylor.
Deebees Gold Penny	B	Mrs D. Beech.
Elspeth Serenade	B	Miss Lomas & Miss Pass.
Macstroud's High Society	B	Mr D. Stroud.
Nelmila Berryfield Beauty	D	Mrs I. M. Millard.
Newholme Marco Polo.	D	Mr W. K. Cherryholme.
Pretty Debbie of Yadnum	B	Miss V. E. Munday.
Star of Keith	D	Mrs I. Copley.
Tayfirs Firegift	D	Mrs J. Fairbrother.
1970		
Blairsville Aristocrat	D	Mr Mrs B. Lister.
Blairsville Shirene	B	Mr & Mrs B. Lister.
Elspeth Nina of Ravaldene	B	Mr V. Ravald.
Lyndoney Timothy Tuppence	D	Mrs E. C. Johnson.
Macstroud's Noble Lad	D	Mr D. Stroud
Murose Wee Pippa	D	Mrs E. Burton.
Skyrona Blue Victoria	B	Mr Sykes.
Super Fine of Yadnum	D	Miss V. E. Munday.

Wykebank Super Solitaire	B	Mr A. Blamires.

1971

Dorrit's Macstroud's Hot Toddy	D	Mrs D. Baynes.
Wykebank Amethyst	B	Mr A. Blamires.
Gaykeys Gold	D	J. & M. Hesketh.
Ravaldene Graybet Rhapsody in Blue	B	Mr V. Ravald.
Brave Warrior of Naylenor	D	Mr P. Naylor.
Chantmarles Bonniface	B	Mrs M. Hayes.
Tolcarne Drambuie	D	Mrs O. Wood.
Blairsville Samantha	B	Mr & Mrs B. Lister.
Deebees Beebee	B	Mrs D. Beech.

1972

Mycariad Ragged Robin of Yadnum	D	Miss V. E. Munday.
Beechrise Surprise	D	Mrs H. Griffiths.
Deanchels Prince Pericles	D	Mrs E. Taylor.
Ozmilion My Imagination	D	Mr O. A. Sameja.
Foxclose Little John	D	Mrs D. M. Jackson.
Kellaylys Miss Sophie	B	Mr J. Thrupp.
Murose Exquisite	B	Mrs E. Burton.
Whisperdales Deebees Halfpenny	B	Mr R. Wardill.

1973

Lloyslee Lass	B	Mr E. Lloyd.
Phirno Lord Gay	D	Miss P. Noakes.
Ozmilion Jubilation	D	Mr O. A. Sameja.
Finstal Sugar Baby	B	Mrs S. Pritchard.
Wykebank Impeccable	B	Mr A. Blamires.
Macstroud's Noble Boy	D	Mr D. Stroud.
Blairsville Most Royale.	B	Mr B. Lister.
Candytops Blue Peter	D	Mr & Mrs Oakley.
Brascaysh Bezzer of Murose	D	Mrs E. Burton.
Chantmarles Saucebox	D	Mrs M. Hayes.

1974

Myork Muffin	D	Mrs K. Kemp.
Jackreed Whisky A Go Go at Stewell	D	Mr & Mrs Bardwell.
Ozmilion Modesty	B	Mr O. A. Sameja.
Foxclose Mr Smartie	D	Mrs M. Jackson.
Deebees Cornish Echo	D	Mrs D. Beech.
Chantmarles Sash Box	B	Mrs M. Hayes.
Robina Gay of Yadnum	B	Miss V. Munday.
Peglea Salamander	B	Mrs P. Foster.
Kellaylys Master Tino	D	Mrs G. Kellar.

1975

Gerjoy Royal Flea	D	Mr G. Wattam.
Clarebecks Moonraker	D	Mrs J. Hughes.
Harleta Uno Go Go	D	Mrs L. Hilton.

Carmardy Little Henry	D	Mr & Mrs Parkin.
Deebees Penny Rose	B	Mrs D. Beech.
Garsims Moonshine	B	Mrs P. Rose.
Naylenor Blue Monarch	D	Mr P. Naylor.
Lyndoney Krishna	D	Mrs D Johnson.
Eburacum Paladin	D	Mr R. Haynes.
Swank of Beechrise	D	Mrs H. Griffiths.
Blairsville Royal Seal	D	Mr & Mrs B Lister.
Macstroud's Soldier Blue	D	Mr D. Stroud.

1976

Katyfare of Candytops	B	Mr & Mrs Oakley.
Ozmilion Justimagine	B	Mr O. A. Sameja.
Empress of Murose	B	Mrs E. Burton.
Toy Top Tango	B	Mrs D. Kitchen.
Candytops Chantilly Lace	B	Mr & Mrs Oakley.
Ozmilion Destiny.	B	Mrs Montgomery.

1977

Peglea Con Tutto	D	Mrs P. Foster.
Ozmilion Distinction	D	Mr O. A. Sameja.
Ozmilion Dream Maker	B	Mrs V. Sameja Williams.
Leadmore Lady Angela	B	Mr W. Cusack.
Chantmarles Elegance	B	Mrs M. Hayes.
Ozmilion Premonition	D	Mr O. A. Sameja.
Wykebank Startime	B	Mr A. Blamire.
Deebees Speculation	D	Mrs D. Beech.
Craigsbank Blue Cinders	B	Mrs J. Mann.
Juliette Bradstara	B	Mr & Mrs Bradshaw.
Chevawn Sweet Shonah	B	Mrs Leyton & Mrs Chiswell.
Candytops Strawberry Fayre	B	Mr & Mrs Oakley.

1978

Shaun of Beechrise	D	Mrs H. Griffiths.
Typros Evening Star	B	Mrs G. Da Silva.
Verolian Justajule with Ozmilion	D	Mrs V. Sameja Hilliard
Ozmilion Exaggeration	B	Mr O. A. Sameja.
Jackreed Appleblossom	D	Mrs J. Reader.
Wellshims Madam of Deebees	B	Mrs Beech & Mrs Shimwell.
Typros The Devil of Spicebox	D	Mrs G. Da Silva.
Naylenor Magic Moment	B	Mr & Mrs P. Naylor.
Candytops Raffles	D	Mr & Mrs Oakley.

1979

Fascination of Daisydell	D	Mr & Mrs M. Turner.
Chantmarles Debutante	B	Mr P. Boot.
Ozmilion Tradition	D	Mr O. A. Sameja.
Wykebank Wild Rose	B	Mrs K. Henderson.
Carmardy Marcus	D	Mr & Mrs Parkin.

Chantmarles Dolly Dimple	B	Mrs M. Hayes.
Deebees My Fascination	D	Mrs Beech & Mrs Shimwell.
Harleta Ferdinando	D	Mr & Mrs Hilton.
Beechrise Sweet Solitaire	B	Mr & Mrs Sargenson.
Chantmarles Stowaway	D	Mrs M. Hayes.
Ozmilion Hearts Desire	B	Mr O. A. Sameja.

1980

Daisydell Tinker	D	Mr & Mrs Kneen.
Mogid Millionairess	B	Mrs M. Giddings.
Craigsbank Miss Dior	B	Mrs J. Mann.
Souvenir of Beechrise	D	Mrs H. Griffiths.
Ozmilion Devotion	D	Mr O. A. Sameja.
Wykebank Tinkerbell	B	Mr A. Blamires.
Chantmarles Proper Madam	B	Mrs M. Hayes.
Deebees Golden Delight	B	Mrs Beech & Mrs Shimwell.
Blairsville Gaiety Boy	D	Mr & Mrs B. Lister.
Murose Illustrious	D	Mrs E. Burton.
Candytops Candy Man	D	Mr & Mrs Oakley.
Ozmilion Ovation	D	Mr O. A. Sameja.

1981

Ozmilion Story of Romance	B	Mr O. A. Sameja.
Johnalenas Silken Charm	D	Mrs K. John.
Finstal Johnathan	D	Mrs S. Pritchard.
Marshonia Blue Secret	D	Mrs P. Robson.
Candytops Fair Delight	B	Mr & Mrs Oakley.
Murose Masterpiece	D	Mrs E. Burton.
Candytops Cavalcadia	D	Mr & Mrs Oakley.
Chandas Shonas Girl	B	Mrs Leyton & Mrs Chiswell.
Franbrin Royal Sapphire of Woodcross	B	Mrs J. Mills.
Chantmarles Rose Bowl	B	Mrs D. Lorenz.
Chantmarles Celebrity	D	Mrs M. Hayes.
Summer Sensation of Sedae	B	Mrs M. Eades.

1982

Stewell Moonstorm	D	Mrs E. Bardwell.
Wykebank Star Choice	B	Mr A. Blamire.
Shipps Shanty Mann	D	Mrs M. Hamill.
Moseville Misty Lady of Hankeyville	B	Mrs Handforth.
Chantmarles Best Intentions	D	Mrs M. Hayes.
Ozmilion Flames of Desire	B	Mr O. A. Sameja.
Relation of Primemeadows	D	Mrs Robinson.
Craigsbank Stormy Affair	B	Mrs J. Leslie.
Jamesons Royal Stewart	D	Mr & Mrs Henderson.
Ozmilion Expectation.	D	Mr O. A. Sameja.
Deebees Dominic	D	Mrs Beech & Mrs Shimwell.
Sharwins Easter Dream	B	Mr D. Baldwin.

1983: Ch. Candytops Royal Cascade (Ch. Candytops Cavalcadia – Candytops Ribbons Delight).
Owned and bred by Mr and Mrs H. Oakley.

Mark Burns.

1986: Ch. Meadpark Silk N Velvet (Meadpark Personality Plus – Meadpark Blue Blaize). Owned and bred by Mr and Mrs Mulligan.

Mark Burns.

Chantmarles Wild Rose	B	Mrs D. Lorenz.
Ozmilion Flames of Passion	B	Mr O. A. Sameja.
Verolian Temptress with Ozmilion	B	Mrs V. Sameja Hilliard.
Wenwytes Whispers Boy	D	Mrs W. White.
1983		
Kindonia Justin	D	Mr & Mrs Briddon.
Ozmilion Love Romance	B	Mr O. A. Sameja.
Arlestry Regal Challenge	D	Mrs E. Howarth.
Ozmilion Invitation	D	Mr O. A. Sameja.
Bee Bee Mi Blaze	B	Mr J. Magri.
Candytops Royal Cascade	D	Mr & Mrs Oakley.
Ozmilion Dance of Romance	B	Mr O. A. Sameja.
1984		
Mondamin My Minstrele	B	Mrs I. Dawson.
Azurene Moss Rose of Yadnum.	B	Miss V. Munday.
Typros Royal Splendour	D	Mrs G. Da Silva.
Emotions of Ozmilion at Rozamie	D	Mr J. Magri.
Naejekin Blue Reflection	D	Mrs E. Carr.
Evening Blue	D	Mr & Mrs Gillespie.
Colletts Charmaine	B	Mrs M. Cole.
Stewells Soul Singer	B	Mr & Mrs Bardwell.
Blairsville Royal Pardon	B	Mr & Mrs Gillespie.
Chantmarles Candy	B	Mr & Mrs Haythornthwaite.
1985		
Ozmilion Hopelessly In Love	B	Mr O. A. Sameja.
Taurusdale Pilinan Hati	D	Mr D. Kee.
Naylenor Crown Jewel	D	Mr & Mrs Naylor.
Craigsbank Sheezalady	B	Mrs J. Leslie.
Yadnum Regal Fare	D	Miss V. E. Munday.
Marshonia Secret Serenade	B	Mrs P. Robinson.
Azurene Corduroy of Yadnum	D	Miss V. E. Munday.
Maritoys Midnight Rose	B	Mrs J. Blamire.
Marshonia Top Secret	D	Mr & Mrs Parker.
Verolian Appreciation at Ozmilion	D	Mrs V. Sameja Hilliard.
Carmardy Cassius	D	Mrs J. Parkin.
1986		
Ozmilion Admiration	D	Mr O. A. Sameja.
Polliam Sweet Delight	B	Mrs P. Osborne.
Shianda Royal Fanfare	D	Mrs S. Davies.
Ozmilion Kisses of Fire	B	Mr O. A. Sameja.
Christmas Fable	B	Mr & Mrs Gillespie.
Keriwell Flirtation	B	Mr J. Wells.
Lovejoys Debonaire Dandy	D	Mrs S. Schaeffer.
Ozmilion Dedication	D	Mr O. A. Sameja.
Verolian The Adventuress at Ozmilion	B	Mrs V. Sameja Hilliard.

1988: Ch. Ozmilion Sensation (Ch. Ozmilion Dedication – Ch. Ozmilion Love Romance). Owned and bred by Mr O. A. Sameja.

Fall.

1988: Ch. Typros Lady of Elegance (Typros Presentation – Massendeans Love in a Mist). Owned and bred by Mrs G. Da Silva.

Hartley.

Lena Alanah Snowdrop of Cyndahl	B	Mrs E. Morris.
Meadpark Silk N Velvet	B	Mr & Mrs Mulligan.
Chandas Inspiration	D	Mrs Leyton & Mrs Chiswell.
1987		
Clantalon Contention	D	Mr & Mrs McKay.
Crosspins Royal Sovereign	B	Mr & Mrs Rigby.
Annlion Love Letter	B	Mrs J. Leslie.
Sladesmark Sweet Allure	B	Mr & Mrs Bursnoll.
Royalties Reflex	D	Mrs Y. Windsor.
Keriwell Reflection	D	Mr & Mrs Wells.
Deanhal Selina	B	Mrs J. Halliday.

1989: Beautara Height of Fashion (Verolian Emporer – Beautara Yours Truly). Owned and bred by Pat Green.

Fall.

Chantmarles President Of Yat	D	Messrs. Downey & Enz.
Carmardy Annie	B	Mrs J. Parkin.
Chantmarles Curiosity	D	Mrs M. Hayes.
Tamiche of Tayfirs	B	Mrs Fairbrother.
Candytops Amelia Fair	B	Mr & Mrs Oakley.
Candytops Royal Sovereign	D	Mr & Mrs Oakley.

1988

Ozmilion Sensation	D	Mr O. A. Sameja.
Kenandee Magic Moment	B	Mrs D. Hurcombe.
Keriwell True Love	B	Mr & Mrs Clelland.
Royal Silk	B	Mr & Mrs Whittaker.
Pittens Whisky Twinkle	D	Mrs H. Ridgewell.
Stradmore Samba	B	Mrs G. Rowland.
Typros Lady of Elegance	B	Mrs G. Da Silva.
Deebees Golden Fancy	B	Mrs Beech & Mrs Shimwell.
Rozamie Endless Love	B	Messrs. Downey & Enz.

1989

Crosspins Royal Brigadier	D	Mr & Mrs Rigby.
Stewell Storm Queen	B	Mr & Mrs Bardwell.
Brybett Finesse	D	Mrs B. Whitbread.
Bananas du Domaine de Monderlay at Gaysteps	B	Mrs A. Fisher.
Chantmarles Chivalry	D	Mrs M. Hayes.
Colletts Gold Sovereign	D	Mrs M. Coles.
Beautara Height of Fashion	B	Mrs P. Green.
Verolian Al Pacino	D	Mrs V. Sameja Hilliard
Chantmarles Gaiety	B	Mrs M. Hayes.

1990: Ch. Kellaylys Miss Cha-Cha of Peglea (Kellaylys Tweedle-dee – Tayfirs Jazz Me Blues of Kellayly). Owned by Peggy Foster, bred by Gwen Kellar.

1990: Ch. Ozmilion Aspect of Love (Ch. Ozmilion Sensation – Ch. Ozmilion Dance of Romance). Owned and bred by Mr O. A. Sameja.

Cyndahl Royal Celebrity	D	Mrs E. Morris.
Chevawn Special Engagement	D	Mrs W. White.
1990		
Ozmilion Infatuation	D	Mr O. A. Sameja.
Ozmilion Irresistable Love	B	Mr O. A. Sameja.
Kellaylys Miss Cha-Cha of Peglea	B	Mrs P. Foster.
Ozmilion Aspect of Love	B	Mr O. A. Sameja.
Pittens Dimple Twinkle	B	Mrs H. Ridgewell.
Beautara Some Charmer	B	Mrs P. Green.

1991: Ch. Jackreed Apple Thyme (Meadpark Personality Plus – Jackreed Uno Jacquelina). Owned and bred by Jacky Reader.

B. Lees.

Davonnes Replica	D	Mrs Y. Windsor.
Clantalon Credentials	D	Mr & Mrs McKay.
Typros New Generation	B	Mrs G. Da Silva.

1991

Colletts Concord	D	Mrs M. Cole.
Gerardene Tomkins	D	Miss M. Anger.
Jackreed Apple Thyme	D	Mrs J. Reader.
Patajohn Magic	D	Mrs P. Allington.
Wenwytes Without a Doubt	D	Mrs W. White.
Yorkfold Johnstounburn Gold Link	D	Mrs D. Hillman.
Lyndoney Love Affaire	B	Mrs D. Johnson.
Ozmilion Started With a Kiss	B	Mr O. A. Sameja.
Shirlines Sovenir of Sedae	B	Mrs M. Eades.

1992

(Up to August 31st)

Baratoba Tell Tale	D	Mr R. Fitzgerald.
Dreamwave Royal Velvet at Shubra	D	Mr & Mrs P. Whitaker.
Ozmilion Illumination	D	Mr O. A. Sameja.
Shirlines Sunsets Serenade	D	Mrs S. Hingley.
Status Quo at Beechrise	D	Mrs H. Griffiths.
Crosspins Mory Kante	B	Mr and Mrs J. Rigby.